D0445053

Eyewitnesses of His Majesty

Eyewitnesses of His Majesty

A First Century Account of the Christ and His Apostles

LOUKAS IATROS
(LUKE THE PHYSICIAN)

A moderized reading of Luke and Acts from the 1599 Geneva Bible
Edited by Eric Rauch

WHITE HALL, WEST VIRGINIA
UNITED STATES OF AMERICA

Eyewitnesses of His Majesty

A First Century Account of the Christ and His Apostles

Printed November 2010

Published & Distributed by:

Tolle Lege Press
46 Mountain Park Drive
White Hall, WV 26554

www.TolleLegePress.com
www.1599GenevaBible.com
800-651-0211

ISBN: 978-0-9831457-0-7

Printed in the United States of America.

Contents

Foreword

For we did not follow cunningly devised fables when we made known to you the power and coming of our Lord Jesus Christ, but were eyewitnesses of His majesty.

II Peter 1:16

THE WORK THAT YOU HOLD IN YOUR HANDS is of inestimable value. Within its pages is the astonishing story of Jesus Christ and the establishment of the Christian Church—an historical account which has changed millions of lives for two millennia. Though scores of books have been written about Jesus and the Christian Church, here in the Gospel of Luke and the Book of Acts we are led *ad fontes*, that is, back to the first-century source concerning the ministry of Christ and His early followers.

Composed sometime between 60-62 AD, this two-volume work (Luke/Acts) was written by a man named Luke (Greek: *Loukas*). In addition to being a devoted follower of Christ, Luke was a missionary, a physician, and a historian. As a Greek from Antioch in Syria, Luke may or may not have been raised with the knowledge of God's Word. What we can be sure of, however, is that at some point in his life he was exposed to the good news of salvation through Jesus Christ, and by grace he believed it. As a "far off" Gentile, Luke was mercifully, through God-given faith, "brought near by the blood of Christ" (Eph. 2:13).

Luke was also a faithful missionary. In fact, we learn from the book of Acts that he traveled with the apostle Paul on his missionary journeys, boldly taking the gospel "to the ends of the earth" (Acts

1:8). The so-called "we" chapters in Acts inform us that Luke was Paul's companion during his perilous travels (see Acts 16, 20-21, 27-28). Moreover, while Paul was imprisoned in Rome and awaiting execution by Emperor Nero, he wrote that "Luke alone" was at his side (II Tim. 4:11). It is quite evident, therefore, that Luke was no half-hearted Christian. Quite the contrary, he risked his very life to spread the life-transforming gospel: the good news that "the Son of Man came to seek and to save the lost" (Luke 19:10).

By trade Luke was a medical doctor. The apostle Paul referred to him as "Luke, the beloved physician" (Col. 4:14). In comparison to the other gospel accounts, Luke's writings are exceptionally descriptive, and this is especially true of his detailed observations of Christ's miracles of healing.

As a first-rate historian, Luke was an excellent student and researcher. Not having witnessed the life and ministry of Christ himself, Luke gathered information like a good investigative reporter from reliable "eyewitnesses" of the ministry of Christ, (the apostles among others) in order to write a well-founded "narrative of the things that have been accomplished among us" (Luke 1:1-4; Acts 1:1; I John 1:1-4). He would have interviewed men such as the apostle John who wrote in his first epistle:

> That which was from the beginning, which we have heard, which we have seen with our eyes, which we looked upon and have touched with our hands, concerning the word of life—the life was made manifest, and we have seen it, and testify to it and proclaim to you the eternal life, which was with the Father and was made manifest to us— that which we have seen and heard we proclaim also to you, so that you too may have fellowship with us; and indeed our fellowship is with the Father and with his Son Jesus Christ. And we are writing these things so that our joy may be complete. (I John 1:1-4)

Commenting on Luke's dependability as a sound historian, a well respected twentieth-century Princeton professor wrote: "Wherever modern scholarship has been able to check up on the accuracy of Luke's work the judgment has been unanimous: he is one of the finest and ablest historians in the ancient world."[1] Furthermore, the preface to Luke's Gospel (v. 1-4) is a superb example of a traditional greeting in classical Greek literature. This, along with the rest of this proficiently written volume, demonstrates that Luke was a highly educated and cultured individual.

Some, of course, will take umbrage at the assertion that reliable history exists at all, believing with Voltaire that "History consists of a series of accumulated imaginative inventions." To be sure, much of history is riddled with distortions. Luke/Acts, however, has all the characteristics of a trustworthy, accurate, historical narrative. Luke wrote this two-volume work to a real person about real events taking place in the lives of real people who lived in real places and had real experiences. Christianity is not built upon erroneous myths or subjective religious feelings, but rather, upon historic, objective facts. If Jesus did not truly live a sinless life, die a substitutionary death and rise victoriously from the grave, then Christianity is a cruel lie, and humanity is without hope (I Cor. 15:17). That is precisely why Luke's factual account of the story of Christ is so marvelous. Redemption has, indeed, been accomplished in Christ!

The initial purpose for the composition of Luke/Acts was to provide a trustworthy account of the life of Christ and of the early church to Theophilus (Luke 1:1-4; Acts 1:1), who was most likely a Roman official and quite possibly a benefactor for Luke's ministry. Theophilus, however, was not meant to be the only recipient of Luke's narrative. Luke/Acts was divinely inspired and set down in writing precisely so that it would be courageously proclaimed to, and joyfully received by, people from every nation—in "Jerusalem, and in all Judea and Samaria, and to the end of the earth" (Acts 1:8; Matt. 28:18-20). From one generation to another—until the end of the age—Luke's narrative was ordained by God to be a beacon of light and truth in a dark and sin-ravaged world.

Dear reader, whether you are a professing believer or simply investigating the Christian faith, I encourage you to read this book with the author's original intent in mind: that you "may have certainty" concerning the truth about Jesus (Luke 1:4).

> *There is salvation in no one else, for there is no other name under heaven given among men by which we must be saved* (Acts 4:12).

Rev. Dr. Jon D. Payne
Minister, Grace Presbyterian Church (PCA)
Douglasville, Georgia
October, 2010

1. Otto Piper, "The Purpose of Luke," *Union Seminary Review* 67.1 (Nov. 1945), 16.

Part One

The Appearance of the Christ

Most noble Theophilus,

Seeing that many have taken it upon themselves to set forth the story of those things—which we are fully persuaded as they have been given to us by those who from the beginning were eyewitnesses and ministers of the word—it seemed good to me also, after I had searched out perfectly all things from the beginning, to write a detailed account for you, so that you might know the certainty of the things of which you have been taught.

In the time of King Herod of Judea, there was a certain priest named Zacharias, of the priestly line of Abijah, who had a wife from the daughters of Aaron, and her name was Elizabeth. Both were just before God and obeyed all the commandments and ordinances of the Lord without fault; and they had no child, because Elizabeth was barren and both were well advanced in age.

It came to pass that as he performed the priest's duty before God, his turn came in order—according to the custom of the priest's office—to burn incense when he went into the temple of the Lord, and a whole crowd of people were outside in prayer while the incense was burning. Then an angel of the Lord appeared to him, standing at the right side of the altar of incense, and when Zacharias saw him, he was terrified and fear fell upon him. But the angel said to him,

"Do not fear Zacharias, for your prayer has been heard and your wife Elizabeth will bear a son and you will call his name John. You will have joy and gladness, and many will rejoice at his birth. He will be great in the sight of the Lord and shall drink neither wine nor strong drink; and he will be filled with the holy Ghost, even from his mother's womb, and he will turn many of the children of Israel to their Lord God. He will go before him in the spirit and power of Elijah, turning the hearts of the fathers to the children and the disobedient to the wisdom of the righteous men, making ready a people prepared for the Lord."

Then Zacharias said to the angel, "How will I know this? For I am an old man and my wife is of a great age." And the angel answered and said to him, "I am Gabriel that stands in the presence of God and I have been sent to speak to you and to tell you this good news. Behold, you shall be mute and not be able to speak until the day that these things take place, because you did not believe my words which shall be fulfilled at the proper time."

Now the people waited for Zacharias, wondering why he delayed so long in the temple. And when he came out, he could not speak to them; then they understood that he had seen a vision in the temple because he made signs to them and remained mute. And it came to pass when the days of his office were finished, that he departed to his own house. And after those days, his wife Elizabeth conceived and hid herself five months, saying, "This is the way the Lord has dealt with me, in the days when he looked on me, to take away my disgrace among men."

In the sixth month, the angel Gabriel was sent from God to a city in Galilee named Nazareth, to a virgin whose name was Mary, who was betrothed to a man whose name was Joseph, from the line of David. And the angel went in to her and said, "Rejoice, favored one, the Lord is with you; blessed are you among women." When she saw him, she was troubled by his words and wondered what type of greeting this was. Then the angel said to her, "Do not fear Mary, because you have found favor with God. Behold, you will conceive in your womb and bear a son and shall call his name Jesus. He will be great and will be called the Son of the most High, and the Lord God shall give to him the throne of his father David, and he will reign over the house of Jacob forever; and of his kingdom there shall be no end."

Then Mary said to the angel, "How shall this happen, since I have not known a man?" And the angel answered and said to her, "The holy Ghost will come upon you, and the power of the most High will overshadow you; therefore also the holy One which shall be born from you will be called the Son of God. And behold, your cousin, Elizabeth, has also conceived a son in her old age. This is now her sixth month—she which was called barren. For with God nothing is impossible." Then Mary said, "Behold, I am the servant of the Lord; let it be done to me according to your word." So the angel departed from her.

Then Mary arose and went quickly into the hill country to a city of Judah, and entered into the house of Zacharias and greeted Elizabeth. And it happened that when Elizabeth heard Mary's greeting, the babe leapt in her belly, and Elizabeth was filled with the holy Ghost. And she cried with a loud voice and said, "Blessed are you among women, because the fruit of your womb is blessed. Why has it been given that the mother of my Lord should come to me? For behold, as soon as the voice of your greeting sounded in my ears, the babe leapt in my belly for joy. And blessed is she that believes because those things which were told her by the Lord shall be done."

Then Mary said, "My soul magnifies the Lord, and my spirit rejoices in God my Savior because he has looked on the poor state of his servant. Behold, from now on all ages will call me blessed, because he that is mighty has done great things for me, and holy is his name. His mercy is from generation to generation to those who fear him. He that showed strength with his arm has scattered the proud in the schemes of their hearts. He has brought down the mighty from their thrones, and has lifted up the lowly. He has filled the hungry with good things, and sent the rich away empty. He has upheld Israel his servant, being mindful of his mercy, just as he has spoken to our fathers, to Abraham and his descendants forever." And Mary stayed with her about three months and afterward returned to her own house.

The Birth of John

Now Elizabeth's time was fulfilled that she was ready to be delivered, and she brought forth a son. Her neighbors and cousins heard it said how the Lord had showed his great mercy upon her, and they rejoiced with her. And so it was that on the eighth day they came to circumcise the child and called him Zacharias, after the name of his father. But his mother answered and said, "No, he shall be called John." And they said to her, "There is no one in your family that has this name." Then they made signs to his father, asking what he would have him called. So he asked for writing tablets and wrote, saying, "His name is John," and they were all amazed. His mouth was immediately opened and with his tongue he spoke and praised God. Then fear came on all of them that lived nearby, and all these words were told abroad throughout all the hill country of Judea. And everyone that heard them pondered in their hearts, saying, "What kind of child is this?" And the hand of the Lord was with him.

Then his father Zacharias was filled with the holy Ghost and prophesied, saying, "Blessed be the Lord God of Israel, because he has visited and redeemed his people. He has raised up the horn of salvation unto us, in the line of his servant David, as he spoke by the mouth of his holy prophets, which since the world began have been saying that he would send us deliverance from our enemies, and from the hands of all that hate us; that he might show mercy toward our fathers and remember his holy covenant and the oath which he swore to our father Abraham, which was that he would grant to us to be delivered out of the hands of our enemies and that we should serve him without fear all the days of our life, in holiness and righteousness before him. And you, child, shall be called the prophet of the most High, for you will go before the face of the Lord to prepare his ways and to give knowledge of salvation to his people by the remission of their sins, through the tender mercy of our God, with which the dayspring from on high has visited us, to give light to those sitting in darkness and in the shadow of death, and to guide our feet into the way of peace." And the child grew and became strong in spirit and remained in the wilderness until the day came that he should reveal himself to Israel.

The Birth of the Christ

And it came to pass in those days that a decree was given by Augustus Caesar that all the world should be taxed. (This first taxing was made when Quirinius was governor of Syria.) Therefore all went to be taxed, every man to his own city. Joseph also went up from Galilee, out of the city called Nazareth, into Judea, to the city of David, which is called Bethlehem (because he was of the house and lineage of David), to be taxed with Mary, who was given to be his wife and was with child.

And so it was that while they were there, the days were completed that she should be delivered, and she brought forth her first begotten son, and wrapped him in swaddling clothes and laid him in a manger, because there was no room for them in the inn. In the same country there were shepherds, abiding in the field, and keeping watch over their flock by night. And behold, the angel of the Lord came upon them, and the glory of the Lord shone about them, and they were very afraid. Then the angel said to them, "Do not be afraid; I bring you good news of great joy that shall be for all the people. Unto you this day is born in the city of David, a Savior, which is Christ the Lord. And this shall be a sign for you: you will find the child swaddled and laying in a manger." And immediately there was a multitude of heavenly soldiers with the angel, praising God and saying, "Glory be to God in the highest heavens, and peace on earth and good will toward men."

When the angels had gone away from them into heaven, the shepherds said to one another, "Let us go to Bethlehem and see this thing that has come to pass, which the Lord has shown to us." So they came quickly and found both Mary and Joseph, and the child was laying in the manger. And when they had seen it, they made known everywhere the thing that was told to them about the child. And all that heard it were amazed by the things the shepherds told them. But Mary kept all those sayings and pondered them in her heart. And the shepherds returned, glorifying and praising God for all that they had heard and seen, as it was spoken to them.

When the eight days were completed, that they should circumcise the child, he was given the name Jesus, which was named by the angel before he was conceived in the womb. And when the days of her purification according to the Law of Moses were finished, they brought him to Jerusalem to present him to the Lord (As it is written in the Law of the Lord: "Every man child that first opens the womb shall be called holy to the Lord.") and to give a sacrifice, as it is commanded in the Law of the Lord: a pair of turtledoves or two young pigeons. And behold, there was a man in Jerusalem whose name was Simeon. He was a just man and feared God and waited for the consolation of Israel, and the holy Ghost was upon him. It was declared to him from God by the holy Ghost, that he should not see death before he had seen the anointed One of the Lord. And he came by the Spirit into the temple when the parents brought the child in to do for him after the custom of the Law. Then he took him in his arms and praised God and said, "Lord, now let your servant depart in peace, according to your word, because my eyes have seen your salvation, which you have prepared before the face of all people; a light to be revealed to the Gentiles and the glory of your people Israel." And Joseph and his mother were amazed by the things which were spoken concerning him. And Simeon blessed them and said to Mary his mother, "Behold, this child is appointed for the fall and rising again of many in Israel and for a sign which shall be spoken against (and a sword shall pierce through your own soul also), so that the thoughts of many hearts may be made known."

There was also a prophetess, Anna the daughter of Phanuel of the tribe of Asher, who was very old. After she had lived with a husband seven years from her virginity, she had been a widow for about eighty-four years, and did not go out of the temple, but served God with fastings and prayers night and day. She came upon them at the same time and likewise confessed the Lord, and spoke of him to all that looked for redemption in Jerusalem. And when they had performed everything according to the Law of the Lord, they returned to Galilee, to their own city of Nazareth. And the child grew and became strong in spirit and was filled with wisdom, and the grace of God was with him.

Now his parents went to Jerusalem every year for the feast of the Passover. When he was twelve years old, they had come up to Jerusalem, and as they were returning, when the custom of the feast and the days there were finished, the child Jesus remained in Jerusalem, and neither Joseph nor his mother knew it. Assuming that he had been among the group, they went a day's journey. When they began to look for him among their family and friends and did not find him, they turned back to Jerusalem and looked for him there. And it came to pass three days later that they found him in the temple, sitting in the midst of the teachers, both hearing them and asking them questions; and all that heard him were astonished at his understanding and answers. So when they saw him they were amazed and his mother said to him, "Son, why have you done this to us? Behold, your father and I have looked for you with very heavy hearts." Then he said to them, "How is it that you were looking for me? Did you not know that I must go about my Father's business?" But they did not understand what he said to them. Then he went down with them and came to Nazareth and was subject to them, and his mother kept all these sayings in her heart. And Jesus increased in wisdom and stature, and in favor with God and men.

A Voice in the Wilderness

Now in the fifteenth year of the reign of Tiberius Caesar—Pontius Pilate being governor of Judea, and Herod being tetrarch of Galilee, and his brother Philip tetrarch of Iturea and of the country of Trachonitis, and Lysanias the tetrarch of Abilene (when Annas and Caiaphas were the high priests)—the word of God came to John, the son of Zacharias in the wilderness. And he came unto all the coasts around Jordan, preaching the baptism of repentance for the remission of sins—as it is written in the book of the sayings of Isaiah the prophet, which says: "The voice of him that cries in the wilderness is, 'Prepare the way of the Lord; make his paths straight. Every valley shall be filled, and every mountain and hill shall be brought low, and crooked things shall be made straight and the rough ways shall be made smooth. And all flesh shall see the salvation of God.'" Then he said to the people that were coming out to be baptized by him, "O generations of vipers, who has forewarned you to flee from the wrath to come? Therefore, bring forth fruits worthy of a repentant life, and do not begin to say among yourselves, 'We have Abraham for our Father,' because I say to you, that God is able to raise up children for Abraham from these stones. Now also is the axe laid at the root of the trees, therefore, every tree which does not bring forth good fruit will be cut down and thrown into the fire."

Then the people asked him, saying, "What shall we do then?" And he answered and said to them, "He that has two coats, let him give to him that has none; and he that has food, let him do likewise." Then there also came tax collectors to be baptized and said to him, "Master, what shall we do?" And he said to them, "Require nothing more than that which is appointed unto you." The soldiers likewise demanded of him, saying, "And what shall we do?" And he said to them, "Do violence to no man. Neither accuse any falsely. And be content with your wages." As the people waited, they all began to debate in their hearts if John were the Christ or not. John answered and said to all of them, "I baptize you with water, but one stronger than me will come, whose shoe's latchet I am not worthy to unloose; he will baptize you with the holy Ghost, and with fire. His fan is in his hand and he will make his threshing floor clean and will gather the wheat into his barn, but the chaff he will burn up with fire that shall never be quenched." Exhorting them with many other things, he preached to the people. But when Herod the tetrarch was rebuked by him for Herodias—his brother Philip's wife—and for all the evils which Herod had done, he added this to them all, and shut John up in prison. Now it came to pass that when all the people were baptized, Jesus was baptized and he prayed. Then the heaven was opened and the holy Ghost came down in a bodily shape like a dove upon him and there was a voice from heaven, saying, "You are my beloved Son, in you I am well pleased."

Jesus himself began his ministry when he was about thirty years of age, being as men supposed the son of Joseph, which was the son of Heli, the son of Matthat, the son of Levi, the son of Melchi, the son of Janna, the son of Joseph, the son of Mattathiah, the son of Amos, the son of Nahum, the son of Esli, the son of Naggai, the son of Maath, the son of Mattathiah, the son of Semei, the son of Joseph, the son of Judah, the son of Joannas, the son of Rhesa, the son of Zerubbabel, the son of Shealtiel, the son of Neri, the son of Melchi, the son of Addi, the son of Cosam, the son of Elmodam, the son of Er, the son of Jose, the son of Eliezer, the son of Jorim, the son of Matthat, the son of Levi, the son of Simeon, the son of Judah, the son of Joseph, the son of Jonan, the son of Eliakim, the son of Melea, the son of Menan, the son of Mattathah, the son of Nathan, the son of David, the son of Jesse, the son of Obed, the son of Boaz, the son of Salmon, the son of Nahshon, the son of Amminadab, the son of Ram, the son of Hezron, the son of Perez, the son of Judah, the son of Jacob, the son of Isaac, the son of Abraham, the son of Terah, the son of Nahor, the son of Serug, the son of Reu, the son of Peleg, the son of Eber, the son of Shelah, the son of Cainan, the son of Arphaxad, the son of Shem, the son of Noah, the son of Lamech, the son of Methuselah, the son of Enoch, the son of Jared, the son of Mahalalel, the son of Cainan, the son of Enosh, the son of Seth, the son of Adam, the son of God.

The Temptation of Jesus

Being full of the holy Ghost, Jesus returned from the Jordan and was led by the Spirit into the wilderness and was tempted there forty days by the devil; and in those days he ate nothing, but when they were ended, he afterward was hungry. Then the devil said to him, "If you are the son of God, command this stone to be made bread." But Jesus answered him, saying, "It is written that man shall not live by bread alone, but by every word of God." Then the devil took him up on a high mountain and showed him all the kingdoms of the world in the twinkling of an eye. And the devil said to him, "All this power will I give you and the glory of those kingdoms, because it is given to me and to whomever I will, I give it. If you therefore will worship me, they shall all be yours." But Jesus answered him and said, "Away from me Satan because it is written, 'You shall worship the Lord your God, and him alone shall you serve.'" Then he brought him to Jerusalem and set him on a pinnacle of the temple and said to him, "If you are the Son of God, throw yourself down from here, because it is written, 'He will give his angels charge over you to keep you; and with their hands they shall lift you up, lest at any time you should strike your foot against a stone.'" And Jesus answered and said to him, "It is said, 'You shall not tempt the Lord your God.'" And when the devil had ended all the temptation, he departed from him for a little while.

Jesus Begins Teaching the People

Jesus returned by the power of the Spirit to Galilee and reports about him were going out throughout the entire region around there; and he taught in the synagogues and was honored of all men. And he came to Nazareth where he had been brought up and as his custom was, he went into the synagogue on the Sabbath day and stood up to read, and the book of the prophet Isaiah was given to him. When he had opened the book, he found the place where it was written: "The Spirit of the Lord is upon me, because he has anointed me, that I should preach the Gospel to the poor. He has sent me, that I should heal the brokenhearted, that I should preach deliverance to the captives and the recovering of sight to the blind, that I should set at liberty them that are bruised, and that I should preach the acceptable year of the Lord." When he closed the book and gave it again to the minister and sat down, the eyes of all that were in the synagogue were fixed on him. Then he began to say to them, "Today is this Scripture fulfilled in your ears." And all bore witness to him and were amazed at the gracious words which proceeded out of his mouth and said, "Is this not Joseph's son?" Then he said to them, "You will surely say to me this proverb, 'Physician, heal thyself,' and whatsoever we have heard done in Capernaum, do it here likewise in your own country." And he said, "Truly I say to you, no prophet is accepted in his own country. But I tell you the truth, there were many widows in Israel in the days of Elijah—when heaven was shut for three years and six months and a great famine was throughout all the land—but unto none of them was Elijah sent except to a certain widow in Zarephath, a city of Sidon. Likewise, many lepers were in Israel in the time of Elisha the prophet, yet none of them was made clean, except Naaman the Syrian." Then all that were in the synagogue were filled with wrath when they heard it and rose up and thrust him out of the city and they led him to the edge of the hill, whereon their city was built, to throw him down headlong. But he passed through the midst of them and went his way and came down into Capernaum, a city of Galilee, and taught there on the Sabbath days. And they were astonished at his doctrine, because he spoke with authority.

In the synagogue there was a man which had a spirit of a demon which cried with a loud voice, saying, "Oh, what have we to do with you, Jesus of Nazareth? Have you come to destroy us? I know who you are, even the Holy one of God." And Jesus rebuked him, saying, "Hold your peace and come out of him." Then the demon, throwing him in the midst of them, came out of him and did not hurt him. So fear came on all of them, and they spoke among themselves, saying, "What is this thing? With authority and power he commands the evil spirits and they come out." And word of him spread everywhere throughout all the places of the country around there.

And he got up and came out of the synagogue and entered into Simon's house. Simon's wife's mother was sick with a great fever and they requested that he come to her. Then he stood over her and rebuked the fever and it left her, and immediately she arose and began serving them.

Now as the sun was setting, all of them that had any who were sick of various diseases brought them to him and he laid his hands on every one of them and healed them. Demons also came out of many, crying and saying, "You are the Christ, the Son of God," but he rebuked them, and did not allow them to say that they knew him to be the Christ. And when it was morning, he departed and went out to a deserted place. The people looked for him and came to him and tried to prevent him from leaving them, but he said to them, "Surely I must also preach the kingdom of God to other cities—this is why I have been sent." So he preached in the synagogues of Galilee.

Then it came to pass that he stood by the lake of Gennesaret, and the people pressed close to him to hear the word of God. He saw two ships standing by the lakeside, but the fishermen had gone out of them and were washing their nets. Then he entered into one of the ships—which was Simon's—and told him that he wanted to be thrust off a little from the land. Then he sat down and taught the people from the ship.

Now when he had finished speaking, he said to Simon, "Launch out into the deep water and let down your nets to make a catch." Then Simon answered and said to him, "Master, we have worked all night and have caught nothing; nevertheless at your word I will let down the net." And when they had done so, they caught a great multitude of fish, so many that their net broke. They called to their partners on the other ship that they should come and help them. When they came, they filled both ships to the point of sinking. When Simon Peter saw this, he fell down at Jesus' knees and said, "Lord, go away from me; I am a sinful man." He was utterly astonished—and all those with him—because of the catch of fish which they took. So also were James and John, the sons of Zebedee, who were companions with Simon. Then Jesus said to Simon, "Fear not, from now on you shall catch men." And when they had brought the ships to land, they left everything and followed him.

It came to pass, as he was in a certain city, that there was a man full of leprosy, and when he saw Jesus, he fell on his face and begged him, saying, "Lord, if you are willing, you can make me clean." So he stretched forth his hand and touched him and said, "I am willing; be clean." Immediately the leprosy departed from him. And he commanded him that he should tell no one. "Go," he said, "and show yourself to the priest and offer your cleansing—as Moses has commanded—for a witness unto them." After this, his fame increased all the more, and great multitudes came together to hear and to be healed by him of their sicknesses. But he kept himself apart in the wilderness and prayed.

It came to pass on a certain day when he was teaching that the Pharisees and teachers of the Law, from every town of Galilee and Judea and Jerusalem sat by, and the power of the Lord was in him to heal them. Then behold, men brought a paralyzed man lying on a bed and they looked for a way to bring him in and to lay him before him. When they could not find a way to bring him in because of the crowd, they went up on the house and let him down through the roof—bed and all—in the midst before Jesus. And when he saw their faith, he said to him, "Man, your sins are forgiven." Then the scribes and the Pharisees began to question, saying, "Who is this that speaks blasphemies? Who can forgive sins but God alone?" But when Jesus perceived their questioning, he answered and said to them, "What are you thinking in your hearts? Which is easier: to say, 'Thy sins are forgiven' or to say, 'Rise and walk?' But so that you may know that the

Son of man has authority to forgive sins on the earth,"—he said to the paralyzed man—"Arise, take up your bed and go into your house." And immediately he got up before them, and took up his bed where he lay and departed to his own house, praising God. And they were all amazed and praised God and were filled with fear, saying, "We have surely seen strange things today."

After this, he went out and saw a tax collector named Levi sitting in the tax booth. He said to him, "Follow me," and he left all, got up, and followed him. Then Levi made him a great feast in his own house, where there was a large gathering of tax collectors and others sitting at the table with them. But those who were scribes and Pharisees were grumbling against his disciples and saying, "Why do you eat and drink with tax collectors and sinners?" Then Jesus answered and said to them, "The ones who are well do not need the physician, but the ones who are sick do. I did not come to call the righteous, but sinners, to repentance." Then they said to him, "Why do the disciples of John fast often and pray, and the disciples of the Pharisees also, but yours are eating and drinking?" And he said to them, "Can you make the wedding guests fast while the bridegroom is still with them? But the days will come, when the bridegroom will be taken away from them; in those days they shall fast." Then he told them this parable: "No man puts a piece of a new garment onto an old one, because then the new garment is torn and the piece taken out of the new does not match the old. Likewise, no man pours new wine into old wineskins because the new wine will burst the wineskins and spill out, and the wineskins will be useless. But new wine must be poured into new wineskins, and so both will be preserved. And no man that drinks old wine immediately desires new. He says, 'The old is better.'"

And it came to pass on another Sabbath that he went through the corn fields and his disciples plucked the ears of corn and rubbed them in their hands and ate. Some of the Pharisees said to them,

"Why are you doing what is not lawful to do on the Sabbath days?" Then Jesus answered them and said, "Have you not read what David did when he was hungry, and those who were with him? How he went into the house of God and took and ate the showbread, and also gave to those who were with him—even though it was not lawful for him to eat, but the priests only?" And he said to them, "The Son of man is Lord also of the Sabbath day."

It also came to pass on yet another Sabbath that he entered into the synagogue and taught, and there was a man whose right hand was withered. And the scribes and Pharisees watched him to see whether he would heal on the Sabbath day, so that they might find an accusation against him. But he knew their intentions and said to the man with the withered hand, "Arise, and stand up in the midst." And he arose and stood up. Then Jesus said to them, "I will ask you a question. Is it lawful on the Sabbath days to do good or to do evil, to save life or to destroy it?" After looking around at all of them, he said to the man, "Stretch out your hand." And he did so and his hand was restored again, as whole as the other. Then they became filled with fury and discussed with one another what they might do to Jesus.

The Calling of the Twelve

And it came to pass in those days that he went to a mountain to pray and spent the night in prayer to God. When it was morning, he called his disciples and of them he chose twelve, which he called apostles: Simon whom he named also Peter and Andrew his brother, James and John, Philip and Bartholomew, Matthew and Thomas, James the son of Alphaeus and Simon called Zealous, Judas James' brother and Judas Iscariot (who also was the traitor). Then he came down with them and stood on a level place with all of his disciples. A great many people out of all Judea and Jerusalem and from the sea coast of Tyre and Sidon had come to hear him and to be healed of their diseases, those who were tormented by unclean spirits were also being healed. And the whole crowd tried to touch him because power went forth from him and healed them all.

And he lifted up his eyes to his disciples and said, "Blessed are you poor, for the kingdom of God is yours. Blessed are you that are hungry, for you shall be filled. Blessed are you that weep now, for you shall laugh. Blessed are you when men hate you and when they exclude you and revile you and put out your name as evil for the Son of man's sake. Rejoice in that day and be glad, for behold your reward is great in heaven, and because this is the same way their fathers received the prophets."

"Woe to you that are rich, for you have received your consolation. Woe to you that are full, for you shall be hungry. Woe to you that now laugh, for you shall wail and weep. Woe to you when all men speak well of you, for likewise did their fathers to the false prophets."

"But I say to those who hear, Love your enemies; do well to them which hate you. Bless them that curse you, and pray for them which hurt you. And to him that strikes you on the one cheek, offer also the other; and to him that takes away your cloak, give him your coat also. Give to every man that asks of you; and of him that takes away the things that belong to you, do not ask to have them back. And as you would have men do to you, so do likewise to them. If you love them which love you, what credit shall you have? Even the sinners love those that love them. And if you do good for them which do good for you, what credit shall you have? Even the sinners do the same. And if you lend to those from whom you hope to receive, what credit shall you have? Even the sinners lend to sinners to receive the same. Therefore love your enemies and do good and lend, looking for nothing in return and your reward shall be great; and you shall be the children of the most High because he is kind to the unkind and to the evil. Therefore be merciful as your Father also is merciful."

"Judge not, and you will not be judged; condemn not, and you will not be condemned. Forgive, and you will be forgiven; give, and it will be given to you—a good measure, pressed down, shaken together and running over shall men pour into your lap. With the measure you use, the same will men use back to you."

And he spoke a parable to them, "Can the blind lead the blind? Shall not both fall into the ditch? The disciple is not above the master, but whosoever is a perfect disciple shall be just like his master. Why do you notice the splinter in your brother's eye, yet ignore the log that is in your own eye? How can you say to your brother, 'Let me pull out the splinter that is in your eye,' when you can't see the log that is in your own eye? You hypocrite, take the log out of your own eye first, and then you will be able to see clearly to take out the splinter that is in your brother's eye."

"A good tree does not bring forth evil fruit, neither does an evil tree bring forth good fruit. Every tree is known by its own fruit, for neither from thorns do men gather figs, nor from bushes do they gather grapes. A good man out of the good treasure of his heart brings forth good; and an evil man out of the evil treasure of his heart brings forth evil. Out of the abundance of the heart his mouth speaks."

"Why do you call me 'Lord, Lord,' and do not do the things that I speak? Whosoever comes to me and hears my words and does them, I will show you to whom he is like: he is like a man which built a house, and dug deep, and laid the foundation on a rock. When the waters arose, the flood beat upon that house and could not shake it, because it was grounded upon a rock. But he that hears and does not, is like a man that built a house upon the earth without foundation, against which the flood did beat, and it fell by and by, and the fall of that house was great."

When he had ended all his sayings in the hearing of the people, he entered into Capernaum. A particular centurion had a servant who was dear to him and who was sick and ready to die. When he heard about Jesus, he sent elders of the Jews to him, begging that he would come and heal his servant. When the elders found Jesus, they quickly began pleading with him, saying, "He is worthy that you should do this for him, because he loves our nation and has built us a synagogue." Then Jesus went with them. But when he was not far from the house, the centurion sent friends to him, saying, "Lord, trouble yourself no longer, for I am not worthy that you should enter under my roof. I did not consider myself to be worthy of coming to you, simply say the word and my servant shall be healed. For I also am a man under authority, having soldiers under me. When I say to one, 'Go,' he goes, and to another, 'Come,' and he comes, and to my servant, 'Do this,' and he does it." When Jesus heard these things he was amazed and turned and said to the people that followed him, "I say unto you, I have not found faith so great in all of Israel." And when they that were sent returned to the house, they discovered the servant was now well.

And it came to pass the next day that he went into a city called Nain, and many of his disciples and a large crowd went with him. When he came near to the gate of the city, behold, there was a dead man being carried out, who was the only begotten son of his mother, who was a widow, and many people from the city were with her. When the Lord saw her, he had compassion on her and said to her, "Do not weep." He went and touched the coffin (and those that carried it stood still) and said, "Young man, I say to you, 'Arise.'" And the man that was dead sat up and began to speak and Jesus brought him to his mother. Then fear came over all of them, and they glorified God, saying, "A great prophet has risen among us, and God has visited his people." And this report of him went forth throughout all Judea and throughout the whole region round about.

Jesus and John

When the disciples of John told him about all these things, John called two of his disciples and sent them to Jesus, saying, "Are you the coming One, or shall we wait for another?" And when the men had come to him they said, "John the Baptist has sent us to you, saying, 'Are you the One that should come, or shall we wait for another?'" At that time, he was curing many of their sicknesses, plagues, and evil spirits, and unto many blind men he had given sight freely. And Jesus answered and said to them, "Go your way and tell John about the things you have seen and heard: the blind see, the lame walk, the lepers are cleansed, the deaf hear, the dead are raised, and the poor receive the Gospel. Blessed is he that shall not be offended by me." When John's messengers had departed, he began to speak to the people about John: "What did you go out into the wilderness to see? A reed shaken by the wind? What then did you go out to see? A man dressed in soft clothing? Behold, they which are gorgeously dressed and live in luxury are in kings' courts. But what did you go out to see? A prophet? Yes, and I tell you, one greater than a prophet. It was about him that it was written, 'Behold, I send my messenger before you which shall prepare the way ahead of you.' For I say unto you, there is no greater prophet than John among those that have been born of women. Nevertheless, he that is the least in the kingdom of God is greater than he."

When all the people and the tax collectors heard this, they accepted God's justice, because they had been baptized by John. But the Pharisees and the teachers of the Law rejected the counsel of God against themselves, because they were not baptized by him. And the Lord said, "To what shall I liken the men of this generation? What thing are they like? They are like little children sitting in the marketplace, crying to one another and saying, 'We have played for you and you have not danced; we have mourned for you and you have not wept.' John the Baptist came neither eating bread, nor drinking wine, and you say, 'He has a devil.' The Son of man comes both eating and drinking, and you say, 'Behold, the man is a glutton and a drinker of wine, a friend of tax collectors and sinners.' But wisdom is justified by all her children."

Then one of the Pharisees desired that Jesus would eat with him, so he went into the Pharisee's house and sat down at the table. And behold, a woman in the city, who was a sinner, when she heard that Jesus was sitting at the table in the Pharisee's house, brought a container of fragrant oil. She stood at his feet behind him weeping, and began to wash his feet with her tears and to wipe them with the hairs of her head, then she kissed his feet and anointed them with the oil. When the Pharisee which invited him saw it, he thought to himself, saying, "If this man were a prophet, he would surely have known what type of woman this is which is touching him, for she is a sinner." Jesus answered and said to him, "Simon, I have something to say to you." And he said, "Say it, teacher."

"There was a particular lender which had two debtors: the one owed five hundred pence, and the other fifty. When they could not pay him back, he forgave them both. Tell me, which of them will love him most?" Simon answered and said, "I suppose the one he forgave the most." And he said to him, "You have judged correctly." Then he turned to the woman and said to Simon, "Do you see this woman? I entered into your house and you gave me no water for my feet, but she has washed my feet with tears and wiped them with the hairs of her head. You gave me no kiss, but since the time I came in she has not ceased kissing my feet. You did not anoint my head with oil, but she has anointed my feet with oil. Therefore I say to you, many sins are forgiven of her because she loved much. To whom a little is forgiven, he loves but a little." And he said to her, "Your sins are forgiven." And those sitting at the table with him began to say to themselves, "Who is this that even forgives sins?" And he said to the woman, "Your faith has saved you, go in peace."

Jesus Teaches in Parables

It came to pass afterward that he went through every city and town, preaching and proclaiming the kingdom of God. The twelve were with him, as were certain women which had been healed of evil spirits and illnesses. There was Mary, who was called Magdalene, out of whom went seven devils; Joanna, the wife of Chuza, Herod's steward; also Susanna, and many others which were providing for him out of their own means. When many people had come unto him out of the cities and gathered together, he told them a parable. "A sower went out to sow his seed, and as he sowed some fell by the wayside and was trampled down and the birds of the air ate it up. And some fell on the stones and when it had sprung up, it withered away because it lacked moisture. And some fell among thorns and the thorns sprang up with it and choked it. And some fell on good ground and sprang up and bore fruit of a hundredfold." And when he had said these things, he cried, "He that has ears to hear, let him hear."

Then his disciples inquired of him, demanding to know what the parable meant. And he said, "Unto you it is granted to know the secrets of the kingdom of God, but to others it is in parables, so that when they see they do not see, and when they hear they do not understand. The parable means this: the seed is the word of God and that which is beside the way are those who hear, but afterward the devil comes and takes away the word from their hearts, lest they should believe and be saved. But that which is on the stones are those who when they have heard it, receive the word with joy, but they have no roots and believe for a little while, but go away in the time of temptation. That which is fallen among thorns are those who have heard and after their departure are choked with cares and with riches and voluptuous living, and bring forth no fruit. But that which fell in good ground are those with an honest and good heart who hear the word and obey it, and bring forth fruit with patience."

"No man when he has lighted a candle covers it with a basket, neither does he put it under the bed, but sets it on a candlestick, that those who enter in may see the light. For nothing is secret that shall not become evident; neither is anything hidden that shall not become known and come to light. Take care therefore how you hear, because whoever has, to him shall it be given, and whoever has not, from him shall be taken even that which it seemed that he had."

Then his mother and his brothers came to him and could not get close to him because of the crowd. Then it was said to him, "Your mother and your brothers are waiting outside and desire to see you." But he answered and said to them, "My mother and my brothers are those which hear the word of God and do it."

It came to pass on a particular day that he went into a ship with his disciples and said to them, "Let us go over to the other side of the lake." After they launched out, he fell asleep as they sailed. Then a storm of wind came down on the lake and they began taking on water and were in danger. Then they went to him and woke him, saying, "Master, Master, we are perishing." And he arose and rebuked the wind and the waves of water and they ceased and it was calm. Then he said to them, "Where is your faith?" Then they feared and wondered among themselves, saying, "Who is this that commands both the winds and water and they obey him?"

So they sailed to the region of the Gadarenes, which is opposite Galilee. And as he went out to land, a certain man from the city met him there who had demons for a long time. He wore no clothing, neither did he live in a house, but among the graves. And when he saw Jesus, he cried out and fell down before him and with a loud voice said, "What have I to do with you, Jesus the son of God the most

High? I beg you not to torment me." He commanded the evil spirit to come out of the man. He had many times been seized and bound with chains and kept in shackles, but he would break the bands and be driven by the demon out into the wilderness. Then Jesus asked him, saying, "What is your name?" He said, "Legion," because many demons had entered into him. And they begged him that he would not command them to go out into the abyss. There was nearby a herd of many pigs feeding on a hill, and the demons begged him that he would allow them to enter into them. So he allowed them. Then the demons left the man and entered into the pigs and the herd rushed down a steep bank into the lake and drowned. When the herdsmen saw what had happened, they fled and told it in the city and in the country. Then the people came out to see what was done and came to Jesus and found the man—out of whom the demons had departed—sitting at the feet of Jesus, clothed and in his right mind, and they became afraid. Those who had seen it told them how he that was possessed by the demons had been healed. Then everyone from the country around the Gadarenes, begged him to depart from them because they were gripped with a great fear, and he went into the ship and returned. Then the man, out of whom the demons had departed, begged him that he might stay with him, but Jesus sent him away, saying, "Return to your own house and show what great things God has done for you." So he went his way and preached throughout the whole city of the great things Jesus had done for him.

And it came to pass when Jesus returned that the people welcomed him, for they all waited for him. And behold, there came a man named Jairus, who was the ruler of the synagogue, and fell down at Jesus' feet and begged him to come to his house because his only daughter—about twelve years of age—was dying. As he went, the people crowded around him. One was a woman with a blood issue for nearly twelve years, who had spent all her money on physicians and none of them could heal her. When she came behind him, she touched the hem of his garment, and immediately her issue of blood stopped. Then Jesus said, "Who is it that has touched me?" When every man denied it, Peter and they that were with him said, "Master, the crowd is surrounding and pressing in on you and yet you say, 'Who has touched me?'" And Jesus said, "Someone has touched me, for I perceive that power has gone out from me." When the woman saw that it was known, she came trembling and fell down before him, and told him before all the people why she had touched him and how she had been healed immediately. And he said to her, "Daughter, be of good cheer; your faith has saved you, go in peace." While he was speaking, there came one from the ruler of the synagogue's house and said to him, "Your daughter is dead; do not trouble the teacher." When Jesus heard it he answered him, saying, "Do not fear; believe and she will be saved." And when he came to the house, he allowed no one to go in with him except Peter, James, John, and the father and mother of the girl. And all were weeping and mourning for her, but he said, "Do not weep, she is not dead but sleeping." And they laughed at him, knowing that she was dead. So he forced them all out, and took her by the hand and cried, saying, "Child, arise." And her spirit returned and she rose immediately, and he commanded that she be given food. Her parents were astonished, but he commanded them to tell no one what had happened.

The Sending of the Twelve

Then he called his twelve disciples together and gave them power and authority over all demons and to heal diseases. He sent them out to preach the kingdom of God and to cure the sick. And he said to them, "Take nothing for your journey, neither staffs, nor bags, neither bread, nor silver, neither take two coats apiece. And any house you enter into, stay there until you depart; and whoever will not receive you, when you leave that city, shake off the very dust from your feet as a testimony against them." And they departed and went through every town, preaching the Gospel and healing.

Now Herod the tetrarch heard of all that was being done by him and he doubted, because it was being said by some that John had risen again from the dead. Some said that Elijah had appeared, and still others said that one of the old prophets had risen again. Then Herod said, "John I have beheaded, who then is this of whom I hear such things?" So he desired to see him.

When the apostles returned, they told him what great things they had done. Then he took them with him and went aside to a solitary place, near to the city called Bethsaida. When the people found out, they followed him and he welcomed them, and spoke to them about the kingdom of God and healed those who had need of healing. And when the day began to wear away, the twelve came and said to him, "Send the people away, that they may go to the towns and villages around here and rest and get food because we are here in a deserted place." But he said to them, "Give them something to eat." And they said, "We only have five loaves and two fishes, unless we should go and buy food for all these people." (There were about five thousand men.) Then he said to his disciples, "Have them sit down by fifties in a group." And they did so, and had everyone sit down. Then he took the five loaves and the two fishes, and looked up to heaven and blessed them, and broke it and gave it to the disciples to set before the people. So everyone ate and was satisfied, and of all that remained twelve baskets full of broken pieces were gathered.

And it came to pass, when he was praying alone that his disciples were with him. He asked them, saying, "Who do the people say that I am?" They answered and said, "John the Baptist, and others say, Elijah, and some say that one of the old prophets has risen again." And he said to them, "But who do you say that I am?" Peter answered and said, "The Christ of God." And he warned and commanded them that they should tell that to no one and said, "The Son of man must suffer many things and be rejected by the elders and the high priests and scribes and be put to death and rise again on the third day."

And he said to all of them, "If any man will come after me, he must deny himself, take up his cross daily, and follow me. For whosoever will save his life, shall lose it; and whosoever shall lose his life for my sake, shall save it. For what will a man benefit if he wins the whole world and destroys or loses himself? For whosoever is ashamed of me and of my words, of him shall the Son of man also be ashamed when he comes in his glory, and in the glory of the Father, and of the holy Angels. And I tell you the truth, some of those standing here shall not taste of death till they have seen the kingdom of God."

And it came to pass about eight days after those words that he took Peter, John, and James and went up to a mountain to pray. As he prayed, the appearance of his face was changed, and his garment became white and glistening. And behold, two men talked with him, who were Moses and Elijah. They appeared in glory and told him of his departure, which would be accomplished at Jerusalem. But Peter and those with him were heavy with sleep, and when they awoke, they saw his glory, and the two men standing with him. And it came to pass, as they departed from him that Peter said to Jesus, "Master, it is good for us to be here; let us therefore make three tabernacles: one for you, one for Moses, and one for Elijah"—not realizing what he was saying. While he was speaking, a cloud came and overshadowed them and they were afraid as they were entering into the cloud. And there came a voice out of the cloud, saying, "This is my beloved Son, hear him." And when the voice had ceased, Jesus was found alone. And they kept silent, telling no man in those days about any of the things which they had seen.

It came to pass on the next day as they came down from the mountain that many people met him. And behold, a man in the crowd cried out, saying, "Master, I beg you, look at my son, for he is all that I have. A spirit has taken him so that he cries out suddenly, and it shakes him so much that he foams at the mouth, and violently departs from him only after it has bruised him. I have begged your disciples to cast him out, but they could not." Then Jesus answered and said, "O faithless and crooked generation, how long shall I be with you and bear with you? Bring your son here." And while he was yet coming, the demon threw him to the ground and shook him. Then Jesus rebuked the unclean spirit and healed the child and delivered him to his father, and they were all amazed at the mighty power of God. While they all wondered about all the things which Jesus did, he said to his disciples, "Mark these words well, for it shall come to pass that the Son of man shall be delivered into the hands of men." But they did not understand what he said because it was hidden from them. Therefore they could not perceive it and were afraid to ask him what he meant.

Then there arose an argument among them about which of them should be the greatest. When Jesus knew the thoughts of their hearts, he took a little child and set him next to him and said to them, "Whosoever receives this little child in my Name, receives me; and whosoever receives me, receives him that sent me. He that is least among you all, he shall be great." And John answered and said, "Master, we saw someone casting out demons in your Name and we forbade him, because he does not follow you with us." Then Jesus said to him, "Do not forbid him, because he that is not against us is with us."

The Sending of the Seventy

It came to pass when the days were competed, that he should be received up, he readied himself fully to go to Jerusalem. He sent messengers ahead of him and they went and entered into a town of the Samaritans to prepare him a place to stay. But they would not receive him because he was determined to go to Jerusalem. When his disciples, James and John, saw it, they said, "Lord, do you want us to command fire to come down from heaven and consume them, just as Elijah did?" But Jesus turned around and rebuked them and said, "You do not know of what spirit you are. For the Son of man has not come to destroy men's lives, but to save them." Then they went to another town, and it came to pass that as they were traveling, a certain man said to him, "I will follow you Lord, wherever you go." And Jesus said to him, "The foxes have holes and the birds of the air have nests, but the Son of man has nowhere to lay his head." He said to another, "Follow me," and the same said, "Lord, allow me first to go and bury my father." And Jesus said to him, "Let the dead bury their dead; you go and preach the kingdom of God." Then another said, "I will follow you Lord, but let me first go and say goodbye to those that are at my house." And Jesus said to him, "No man that puts his hand to the plow and looks back is suitable for the kingdom of God."

After these things, the Lord appointed seventy more and sent them, in pairs, ahead of him into every city and place where he himself should come. And he said to them, "The harvest is plentiful, but the laborers are few; pray therefore that the Lord of the harvest will send forth laborers into his harvest. Go your way and recognize that I am sending you out as lambs among wolves. Take neither a bag, nor money, nor shoes, and greet no man along the way. Whichever house you enter, first say, 'Peace be upon this house.' And if a son of peace is there, your peace shall rest upon him; if not, it shall return to you. Remain in that house, eating and drinking the things they set before you, because the laborer is worthy of his wages. Do not go from house to house. But into whatever city you enter, if they receive you, eat the things that are set before you and heal the sick that are there and say to them, 'The kingdom of God has come near to you.' But into whatever city you enter, if they will not receive you, go your way into the streets and say, 'Even the very dust which clings to us from your city, we wipe off against you, because you did not know that the kingdom of God had come near to you.' For I tell you, it shall be easier in that day for the people of Sodom than for that city. Woe to you, Chorazin. Woe to you, Bethsaida. If the miracles had been done in Tyre and Sidon which have been done in you, they would have a long time ago repented, sitting in sackcloth and ashes. Therefore, it shall be easier for Tyre and Sidon at the judgment than for you. And you, Capernaum, which is exalted to heaven, shall be thrown down to hell. He that listens to you listens to me, he that hates you hates me, and he that hates me hates him that sent me."

When the seventy returned, they proclaimed with joy, "Lord, even the demons submit to us through your Name." And he said to them, "I saw Satan, like lightning, fall down from heaven. Behold, I have given you the power to tread on serpents and scorpions and over all the power of the enemy and nothing shall hurt you. Even so, don't rejoice because the spirits are submitting to you; instead, rejoice because your names are written in heaven." That same hour, Jesus rejoiced in the spirit and said, "I confess to you, Father, Lord of heaven and earth, that you have hidden these things from the wise and knowing, and have revealed them to children. Even so, Father, because it has pleased you, all things have been given to me by my Father. No one knows who the Son is except the Father, neither who the Father is except the Son, and the one to whom the Son will reveal him."

Then he turned to his disciples and said privately, "Blessed are the eyes that see what you have seen. I tell you that many prophets and kings have desired to see what you have seen, yet have not seen them, and to hear the things which you have heard, yet have not heard them."

Then behold, a certain lawyer stood up and questioned him, saying, "Master, what shall I do to inherit eternal life?" And he said to him, "What is written in the Law? How does it read to you?" And he answered and said, "You shall love the Lord God with all your heart and with all your soul and with all your strength and with all your thoughts, and your neighbor as yourself." Then he said to him, "You have answered correctly; do this and you shall live." But wanting to justify himself, he said to Jesus, "Who then is my neighbor?" And Jesus answered and said, "A certain man went down from Jerusalem to Jericho and fell among thieves, and they stripped him of his clothing and assaulted him and departed, leaving him half-dead. Now it happened that there came down a certain priest that same way, and when he saw him, he passed by on the other side. Likewise also a Levite, when he had come near to the place, went and looked on him, and passed by on the other side. Then a certain Samaritan was on a journey and came near to him, and when he saw him, he had compassion on him. He went to him and bound up his wounds, pouring on oil and wine, and set him on his own animal and brought him to an inn and took care of him. The next morning, when he departed, he took out two pence and gave them to the innkeeper and said to him, 'Take care of him and whatever more you spend, when I come again, I will repay you.' Now which of these three do you think was a neighbor to him that fell among the thieves?" And he said, "The one that showed mercy to him." Then Jesus said to him, "Go and do likewise."

Now it came to pass that as they went, he entered into a certain town and a certain woman named Martha received him into her house. She had a sister named Mary, which also sat at Jesus' feet and listened to his preaching. But Martha was distracted by all of the serving, and came to him and said, "Master, do you not care that my sister has left me to serve everyone alone? Tell her to help me." And Jesus answered and said to her, "Martha, Martha, you worry and are troubled by many things, but one thing is necessary. Mary has chosen the good part, which shall not be taken away from her."

The Lord's Prayer

And so it was, when he was praying in a certain place and had finished, one of his disciples said to him, "Lord, teach us to pray, as John also taught his disciples." And he said to them, "When you pray, say, 'Our Father who is in heaven, hallowed be your Name. Your kingdom come, your will be done, even in earth, as it is in heaven. Our daily bread give to us each day, and forgive us of our sins, for we forgive every man that is indebted to us, and lead us not into temptation, but deliver us from evil.'"

He also said to them, "Which of you has a friend and would go to him at midnight and say to him, 'Friend, lend me three loaves because a friend of mine has arrived from a journey and I have nothing to set before him.' And from inside he answers and says, 'Do not trouble me; the door is now shut and my children are with me in bed. I cannot rise and give them to you.' I say to you that though he would not arise and give them to him because he is a friend, yet because of his persistence, he will rise and give him as many as he needs. Likewise, I say to you, ask and it shall be given to you, seek and you shall find, knock and it shall be opened to you. Everyone that asks, receives; and he that seeks, finds; and to him that knocks, it shall be opened. If a son shall ask for bread from any of you that is a father, will you give him a stone? Or if he asks for a fish, will you give him a serpent? Or if he asks for an egg, will you give him a scorpion? If you then, being evil, can give good gifts to your children, how much more shall your heavenly Father give the holy Ghost to them that desire him?"

Then he cast out a demon which was mute, and when the demon was gone out, the mute man spoke and the people were amazed. But some of them said, "He is casting out demons through Beelzebub, the ruler of the demons." Others tempted him, asking for a sign from heaven. But he knew what they were thinking and said to them, "Every kingdom divided against itself shall be destroyed, and a divided household will fall. So if Satan also is divided against himself, how then shall his kingdom stand, because you are saying that I cast out demons through Beelzebub? If I cast out demons through Beelzebub, by whom do your children cast them out? Therefore they shall be your judges. But if I cast out demons by the finger of God, surely the kingdom of God has come unto you. When a strong man is armed, his palace and the things he owns are kept in peace. But when a stronger man comes upon him and overpowers him, he takes from him all his armor in which he trusted and divides the plunder. He that is not with me is against me; and he that does not gather with me, scatters. When the unclean spirit is gone out of a man, he walks through dry places, seeking rest. When he finds none, he says, 'I will return to the house from where I came.' And when he returns, he finds it swept and ordered. Then he goes and finds seven other spirits, worse than himself, and they enter in and live there, so the last state of that man is worse than the first."

And it came to pass as he said these things that a certain woman in the crowd lifted up her voice and said to him, "Blessed is the womb that bore you and the breasts from which you nursed." But he said, "Blessed instead are those that hear the word of God and obey it."

As the crowd kept getting larger, he began to say, "This is a wicked generation because they seek a sign, but no sign shall be given to them except the sign of Jonah the prophet. Just as Jonah was a sign to the Ninevites, so shall the Son of man also be to this generation. The Queen of the South shall rise up in judgment and condemn the men of this generation, because she came from the remote parts of the earth to listen to the wisdom of Solomon, and behold, something greater than Solomon is here. The men of Nineveh shall rise up in judgment and condemn this generation because they repented at the preaching of Jonah, and behold, something greater than Jonah is here. No man after he has lighted a candle puts it in a hidden place, neither under a basket but on a candlestick, so that they which come in may see the light. The light of the body is the eye, therefore when your eye is pure, then is your whole body full of light; but if your eye is evil, then your body is full of darkness. Therefore, be careful that the light which is in you is not darkness. If therefore your whole body is full of light, having no part darkened, then shall everything be bright, as it is when a candle gives light to you with its brightness."

As he spoke, a certain Pharisee asked him to dine with him, and he went in and sat down at the table. When the Pharisee saw it, he was astonished that he had not first washed before dinner. And the Lord said to him, "Indeed, you Pharisees make the outside of the cup and the dish clean, but inside you are full of greed and wickedness. You fools, did not he that made the outside make the inside also? Therefore, give freely of the things which you have, and behold, all things shall be clean unto you. Woe to you, Pharisees, because you tithe the mint and the rue and every kind of herb, but you disregard the justice and love of God. These you ought to have done, while not leaving the others undone. Woe to you, Pharisees, because you love the highest seats in the synagogues, and greetings in the marketplaces. Woe to you, scribes and Pharisees, hypocrites! You are like unmarked graves, which men walk over without knowing it."

Then one of the lawyers answered and said to him, "Master, by saying this, you are also rebuking us." And he said, "Woe to you also, lawyers; you load men with burdens too heavy to be carried, but you yourselves will not even touch the burdens with one of your fingers. Woe to you, because you build the tombs for the prophets whom your fathers killed. Truly you are witnesses and approve of the deeds of your fathers because they killed them and you are building the tombs. Therefore, said the wisdom of God, 'I will send them prophets and apostles, whom they will kill and persecute,' so that the blood of all the prophets shed from the foundation of the world, may be required of this generation. From the blood of Abel to the blood of Zechariah—who was slain between the altar and the temple—truly I say to you, it will be required of this generation. Woe to you, lawyers, because you have taken away the key of knowledge. You did not enter in yourselves, and you prevented others from entering." When he had said these things to them, the scribes and Pharisees began to press him and to provoke him to speak of many other things; lying in wait for him, looking for something he said that they could use to accuse him.

In the meantime, the crowd grew to be many thousands of people, so that they were trampling one another, and he began to say to his disciples first, "Be careful of the leaven of the Pharisees, which is hypocrisy. Nothing is covered that shall not be revealed, nor hidden that shall not be known. Therefore whatsoever you have spoken in darkness shall be heard in the light, and that which you have whispered in secret places shall be preached from the rooftops. I say to you, my friends, do not be afraid of them that kill the body and after that are able to do nothing more. But I will warn you whom you should fear. Fear him who after he has killed, has the power to cast into hell. Yes, I tell you, fear him."

"Are not five sparrows bought for two farthings, and yet not one of them is forgotten before God? Yes, and all the hairs of your head are numbered. Do not fear therefore, you are of more value than many sparrows. I also say to you that whosoever confesses me before men, him shall the Son of man also confess before the angels of God. But he that denies me before men shall be denied before the angels of God. And whosoever shall speak a word against the Son of man, it shall be forgiven him; but to him that blasphemes the holy Ghost, it shall not be forgiven. And when they bring you into the synagogues and before the rulers and princes, give no thought to how or what you will answer, or what you will say. The holy Ghost shall teach you in that very hour what you are to say."

Then someone in the crowd said to him, "Master, tell my brother to divide the inheritance with me." And he said to him, "Man, who made me a judge or arbitrator over you?" Then he said to them, "Take heed and beware of covetousness, for even though a man may have much, his life does not consist of his riches." And he spoke a parable to them, saying, "The ground of a certain rich man brought forth many fruits. Therefore he thought to himself, saying, 'What shall I do, because I have no more room where I may store up my fruits?' And he said, 'This is what I will do: I will tear down my barns and build bigger ones, and that is where I will store all my fruits and goods. And I will say to my soul, "Soul, you have many goods stored up for many years; live in leisure. Eat, drink, and be merry."' But God said to him, 'You fool, tonight they will take away your soul from you; who shall own those things which you have prepared?' So is he that gathers riches to himself, but is not rich in God."

Then he spoke to his disciples, "Therefore I say to you to not worry about your life and what you will eat, neither for your body and what you will wear. Life is more than food and the body more than clothing. Consider the ravens, they neither sow nor reap; neither do they have storehouses nor barns, and yet God feeds them. How much more valuable are you than birds? And which one of you, by worrying, can add one cubit to his height? If you are then not able to do these small things, why do you worry about the others? Consider the lilies, how they grow. They neither labor nor spin; yet I say to you, that Solomon himself in all his royalty was not clothed like one of them. If God then so clothes the grass, which is in the field today and tomorrow is thrown into the furnace, how much more will he clothe you? You men of little faith! Do not seek what you shall eat or what you shall drink, and do not continue worrying. For all these types of things are what the people of the world seek and your Father knows that you need them. Instead, seek the kingdom of God and all these things shall be given to you. Do not fear, little flock, because it is your Father's pleasure to give you the kingdom. Sell what you have and give to the needy. Make purses for yourselves that will not wear out, a treasure in heaven that can never fail, where neither thief comes near nor moth destroys. For where your treasure is, there will your heart be also."

"Keep yourselves dressed, with your lamps burning. Be like men that wait for their master to return from the wedding feast, so that when he comes and knocks, they may immediately open it for him. Blessed are those servants whom the Lord finds awake when he comes. Truly I say to you, he will dress himself and make them to sit down at the table, and will come forth and serve them. Even if he comes in the second watch, or in the third watch, and shall find them so, those servants are blessed. Now understand this, if the head of the house had known when the thief was coming, he would have watched and would not have allowed his house to be broken into. Therefore, you also be prepared because the Son of man will come at an hour when you do not expect it." Then Peter said to him, "Master, are you telling this parable to us, or to everyone?" And the Lord said, "Who is a faithful and wise steward, one whom the master shall make a ruler over his household and give a portion of food at the proper time? Blessed is that servant, whom his master shall find so doing when he comes. Truly I say to you, that he will make him ruler over everything that he has. But if that servant should say in his heart, 'My master has delayed his coming,' and shall begin to beat the servants and the women, and to eat and drink and to be drunken, then the master of that servant will come on a day he does not expect, and at an hour he does not know, and will cut him to pieces and give him a place with the unbelievers. Also, the servant that knew his master's will and did not prepare himself, neither did according to his will, he shall receive many lashes. But he that did not know and yet did things worthy of punishment, he shall be beaten with few lashes. For to whom much is given of him shall be much required; and to whom men have entrusted much the more they will demand of him."

"I have come to bring fire upon the earth, and how I wish it were already kindled. Nevertheless, I must be baptized with a baptism, and great is my distress until it is finished. Do you think that I have come to bring peace on the earth? I tell you, no, but rather division. From now on, there shall be five in one house divided: three against two, and two against three. The father shall be divided against the son, and the son against the father; the mother against the daughter, and the daughter against the mother; the mother-in-law against her daughter-in-law, and the daughter-in-law against her mother-in-law."

Then he said to the people, "When you see a cloud rise in the west, immediately you say, 'A shower is coming,' and so it is. And when you see the south wind blow, you say, 'It will be hot,' and it comes to pass. Hypocrites, you can discern the face of the earth and of the sky, but why can you not discern the time? Yes, and why can you not judge for yourselves what is right? While you are going with your adversary to stand before the judge, while you are walking, be diligent to be reconciled to him, so that he will not drag you before the judge, because the judge will hand you to the jailer and the jailer will throw you in prison. I tell you, you shall not depart from there until you have paid the very last mite."

The Kingdom of God

There were some men present at that same time that told him about the Galileans, whose blood Pilate had mingled with their sacrifices. Jesus answered and said to them, "Do you suppose that these Galileans were greater sinners than all the other Galileans, because they have suffered such things? I tell you, no; but unless you repent, you will all likewise perish. Or do you think that those eighteen, upon whom the tower in Siloam fell and killed, were sinners more than men that dwell in Jerusalem? I tell you, no; but unless you repent, you will all likewise perish."

He also told this parable, "A certain man had a fig tree growing in his vineyard, and he came and looked for fruit on it and found none. Then he said to the keeper of his vineyard, 'Behold, for three years I have come and looked for fruit on this fig tree, and have found none. Cut it down; why allow it to use up the ground?' And he answered and said to him, 'Lord, leave it alone this year also, until I dig around about it and fertilize it. Then if it bears fruit, good, and if not, then you can cut it down.'"

Then he taught in one of the synagogues on the Sabbath day. And behold, a woman was there which had a spirit of sickness for eighteen years; she was bent over and could not straighten herself up at all. When Jesus saw her, he called her to him and said to her, "Woman, you are freed from your disease." And he laid his hands on her and immediately she stood up straight again and glorified God. And the ruler of the synagogue was indignant because Jesus had healed on the Sabbath day and said to the people, "There are six days in which men ought to work, therefore come in then and be healed, not on the Sabbath day." Then the Lord answered him and said, "Hypocrite, does not each one of you on the Sabbath day let his ox or his donkey out of its stall and lead him away to the water? Then should not this daughter of Abraham, whom Satan kept bound for eighteen years, be freed from this bond on the Sabbath day?" And after he said these things, all his adversaries were ashamed, but all the people rejoiced at all the excellent things being done by him.

Then he said, "What is the kingdom of God like? To what shall I compare it? It is like a grain of mustard seed, which a man took and sowed in his garden; and it grew, and became a great tree, and the birds of the air made nests in its branches." Again he said, "To what shall I compare the kingdom of God? It is like leaven, which a woman took and mixed into three pecks of flour until all of it was leavened." And he went through all the cities and towns, teaching and journeying towards Jerusalem.

Then someone said to him, "Lord, are there few that will be saved?" And he said to them, "Strive to enter in at the narrow gate, because I tell you that many will seek to enter in and shall not be able. When the head of the house gets up and shuts the door, you will begin to stand outside and knock on the door, saying, 'Lord, Lord, open for us.' Then he shall answer and say to you, 'I do not know from where you have come.' Then you shall say, 'We have eaten and drunk in your presence, and you have taught in our streets.' But he shall say, 'I tell you, I do not know from where you have come; depart from me, all you workers of evil.' Then there shall be weeping and gnashing of teeth; you shall see Abraham, Isaac, and Jacob, and all the prophets in the kingdom of God, yet you will be thrust out the doors. Then shall come many from the east and from the west, and from the north and from the south, and shall sit at the table in the kingdom of God. And behold, there the last shall be first, and the first shall be last."

The same day, certain Pharisees came and said to him, "Depart and leave here, because Herod wants to kill you." Then he said to them, "You go and tell that fox, 'Behold, I cast out demons and will continue healing today and tomorrow, and the third day I shall be finished.' Nevertheless, I must travel today and tomorrow and the day following, because it cannot be that a prophet should perish outside of Jerusalem. O Jerusalem, Jerusalem, which killed the prophets and stoned them that were sent to you; how often would I have gathered your children together, as the hen gathers her chicks under her wings, but you were unwilling. Behold, your house is left unto you desolate. I tell you the truth, you shall not see me until the time comes when you will say, 'Blessed is he that comes in the name of the Lord.'"

And it came to pass that when he had entered into the house of one of the chief Pharisees on the Sabbath day to eat bread, they were closely watching him. And behold, there was a certain man before him which had much swelling. Then Jesus spoke to the lawyers and Pharisees, saying, "Is it lawful to heal on the Sabbath day?" And they held their peace. Then he took him and healed him and let him go. He answered them, saying, "Which of you shall have a donkey or an ox that falls into a pit, and will not immediately pull him out on the Sabbath day?" And they could not answer him again to those things.

He also told a parable to the guests, when he saw how they were choosing out the places of honor and said to them, "When you shall be invited by any man to a wedding, do not set yourself down in the highest place, lest a more honorable man than yourself has also been invited, and he that invited both shall say to you, 'Give this man your place,' and then you will be shamed to take the lower place. Rather, when you are invited, go and sit down in the lowest place, so that when he that invited you shall come, he may say to you, 'Friend, sit up higher.' Then you will have honor in the presence of all them that sit at the table with you. For whosoever exalts himself shall be humbled, and he that humbles himself shall be exalted."

Then he also said to him that had invited him, "When you make a dinner or a supper, do not call your friends, nor your brothers, neither your family, nor the rich neighbors, because they may also invite you and this will be your repayment. But when you have a feast, call the poor, the maimed, the lame and the blind, and you will be blessed, because they cannot repay you; you will be repaid at the resurrection of the righteous."

Now when one of them that sat at the table heard these things, he said to him, "Blessed is he that eats bread in the kingdom of God." Then he said to him, "A certain man made a great feast and invited many. He sent his servant at supper time to say to them that were invited, 'Come, for all things are now ready.' But all of them together began to make excuses. The first said to him, 'I have bought a farm and need to go out and see it. Please allow me to be excused.' And another said, 'I have bought five yoke of oxen and I must go examine them. Please allow me to be excused.' And another said, 'I have married a wife and therefore I cannot come.' Then the servant returned and told his master about these things. Then the head of the house became angry and said to his servant, 'Go out quickly into the streets and alleys of the city and bring the poor in here, and the maimed, and the lame, and the blind.' And the servant said, 'Lord, it is done as you have commanded, and there is still room.' Then the master said to the servant, 'Go out into the highways and hedges, and compel them to come in, so that my house may be filled. For I say to you, none of those men which were invited, shall taste of my supper.'"

Now a crowd of many accompanied him, and he turned and said to them, "If any man comes to me and does not hate his father, and mother, and wife, and children, and brethren, and sisters, yes, even his own life, he cannot be my disciple. And whosoever does not take up his cross and come after me, cannot be my disciple. For which of you, if you want to build a tower, will not sit down first and count the cost, to know whether he has enough to finish it? Otherwise, after he has laid the foundation and is not able to complete it, all that behold it will mock him, saying, 'This man began to build, and was not able to finish.' Or what king, before going to make war against another king, does not first sit down and take counsel, considering whether he is able with ten thousand to meet him who comes against him with twenty thousand? Or else, while he is still a far way off, he will send an ambassador and ask for peace. Likewise, any one of you that will not forsake all that he has cannot be my disciple. Salt is good, but if salt loses its flavor, how shall it be salted? It is neither good for the land nor for the dunghill, men throw it out. He that has ears to hear, let him hear."

Then all the tax collectors and sinners were drawing near to hear him. Therefore the Pharisees and scribes grumbled, saying, "He welcomes sinners and eats with them." Then he told this parable to them, saying, "What man among you, having a hundred sheep, if he should lose one of them, would not leave the ninety-nine in the wilderness, and go after that which was lost until he finds it? And when he has found it, he lays it on his shoulders with joy. And when he comes home, he calls together his friends and neighbors, saying to them, 'Rejoice with me; for I have found my sheep which was lost.' I say to you, that same joy shall be in heaven for one sinner that repents, more than for ninety-nine righteous men which need no repentance. Or what woman having ten coins, if she loses one coin, does not light a candle and sweep the house, searching diligently until she finds it? And when she has found it, she calls her friends and neighbors, saying, 'Rejoice with me; for I have found the coin which I had lost.' Likewise I say to you, there is joy in the presence of the angels of God for one sinner that repents." Then he said, "A certain man had two sons and the younger of them said to his father, 'Father, give me the share of the estate that is mine.' So he divided his wealth between them. Not many days later, when the younger son had gathered everything together, he traveled to a far country and there he wasted his money with reckless living. Now when he had spent everything, there arose a great famine throughout that land and he began to be in need. Then he went and became a servant to a citizen of that country, and he sent him to his farm to feed the pigs. And he wanted to fill his belly with the husks that the swine ate, but no man gave them to him. When he came to himself, he said, 'How many hired servants at my father's have enough bread, and I am dying of hunger? I will rise and go to my father and say to him, "Father, I have sinned against heaven, and before you. I am no more worthy to be called your son; make me like one of your hired servants."' So he arose and came to his father and when he was still a long way off, his father saw him and had compassion, and ran and embraced him and kissed him. And the son said to him, 'Father, I have sinned against heaven, and before you, and am no more worthy to be called your son.' Then the father said to his servants, 'Bring out the best robe and put it on him, put a ring on his hand and shoes on his feet; bring the fatted calf and kill him, and let us eat and be merry. For my son was dead and is alive again; he was lost but he is found.' And they began to be merry. Now the older brother was in the field and when he came near to the house, he heard music and dancing and called one of his servants and asked what those things meant. And he said to him, 'Your brother has come and your father has killed the fatted calf, because he has received him safe and sound.' Then he became angry and would not go in. Therefore his father came out and pleaded with him. But he answered and said to his father, 'Look, these many years have I served you, neither did I disobey your commands, yet you never gave me a calf that I might make merry with my friends. But when your son has come, which has devoured your money with harlots, you have for his sake killed the fatted calf.' And he said to him, 'Son, you are always with me and all that I have is yours. It was proper that we should make merry and be glad, because your brother was dead and is alive again. He was lost, but he is found.'"

And he also said to his disciples, "There was a certain rich man who had a steward and he was being accused of wasting his goods. And he called him and said to him, 'What is this I am hearing of you? Give an account of your stewardship, because you may no longer be a steward.' Then the steward said to himself, 'What shall I do since my master is taking away from me the stewardship? I cannot dig and to beg would be shameful. I know what I will do. When I am put out of the stewardship, they will welcome me into their houses.' Then he called all of his master's debtors to him and said to the first, 'How much do you owe to my master?' And he said, 'A hundred measures of oil.' And he said to him, 'Take your bill and sit down quickly and write fifty.' Then he said to another, 'How much do you owe?' And he said, 'A hundred measures of wheat.' Then he said to him, 'Take your bill and write eighty.' And his master commended the unjust steward because he had done wisely. Therefore the children of this world are in their generation wiser than the children of light. And I tell you to make friends for yourselves with the riches of unrighteousness, so that when it fails, they may receive you into eternal dwellings. He that is faithful in little is also faithful in much, and he that is unjust in a little is also unjust in much. If then you have not been faithful with the riches of unrighteousness, who will trust you with the true treasure? If you have not been faithful with another man's goods, who will give to you that which is your own? No servant can serve two masters; either he will hate the one and love the other, or else he will lean to the one and despise the other. You cannot serve God and riches."

Now the Pharisees, who were lovers of money, heard all these things and they scoffed at him. Then he said to them, "You are the ones which justify yourselves before men, but God knows your hearts, that which is highly praised among men, is an abomination in the sight of God. The Law and the Prophets lasted until John, and since that time the kingdom of God is preached and every man presses into it. Now it is easier for heaven and earth to pass away, than for one letter of the Law to fail. Whosoever puts away his wife and marries another commits adultery, and whosoever marries her that is put away from her husband commits adultery."

"There was a certain rich man, always clothed in purple and fine linen, who feasted sumptuously every day. There was also a certain beggar, named Lazarus, who was laid at his gate and was full of sores, desiring to be fed by the crumbs that fell from the rich man's table, yes, and the dogs came and licked his sores. And so it was that the beggar died and was carried by the angels into Abraham's bosom. The rich man also died and was buried. And being tormented in hell, he lifted up his eyes and saw Abraham far away and Lazarus in his bosom. Then he cried out and said, 'Father Abraham, have mercy on me. Send Lazarus that he may dip the tip of his finger in water and cool my tongue, because I am tormented in this flame.' But Abraham said, 'Son, remember that in your lifetime you received your pleasures, and likewise Lazarus received pains; now he is therefore comforted and you are tormented. Besides all this, between you and us there has been set a great chasm, so that they which would go from here to you are not able, neither can they come from there to us.' Then he said, 'I beg you therefore father, send him to my father's house, because I have five brothers, so that he may testify to them, or else they will also come into this place of torment.' Abraham said to him, 'They have Moses and the Prophets, let them hear them.' And he said, 'Not so, father Abraham, but if someone came to them from the dead, then they would repent.' But he said to him, 'If they hear not

Moses and the Prophets, neither will they be persuaded, even by one rising again from the dead.'"

Then he said to his disciples, "It cannot be avoided that temptations will come, but woe to him by whom they come. It would be better for him if a great millstone were hanged around his neck and he were cast into the sea, than that he should offend one of these little ones. Take heed to yourselves. If your brother sins against you, rebuke him; if he repents, forgive him. And even if he sins against you seven times in a day, and seven times in a day he turns to you again and says he repents, you shall forgive him."

And the apostles said to the Lord, "Increase our faith." And the Lord said, "If you had faith, as much as a grain of a mustard seed, and should say to this mulberry tree, 'Pick yourself up by the roots and plant yourself in the sea,' even it will obey you. Who among you, if you have a servant plowing or feeding cattle, would say to him when he has come in from the field, 'Go, and sit down at the table'? Rather would you not say to him, 'Prepare something for me to eat, and dress yourself and serve me; when I have finished eating and drinking, afterward you may eat and drink'? Does he thank the servant, because he did that which he was commanded to do? I think not. Likewise, when you have done all the things which are commanded to you, say, 'We are unworthy servants; we have done that which was our duty to do.'"

Jesus Nears Jerusalem

And so it was that as he went to Jerusalem that he passed between Samaria and Galilee. And as he entered into a certain town, ten men that were lepers met him there, and stood a far way off. They raised their voices and said, "Jesus, Master, have mercy on us." And when he saw them, he said to them, "Go, show yourselves to the priests." And it came to pass that as they went, they were cleansed. One of them, when he saw that he was healed, turned back, and with a loud voice praised God and fell down on his face at his feet, giving him thanks. And he was a Samaritan. Jesus answered and said, "Were not ten cleansed? Where are the nine? Is there none found that returned to give God praise, except this foreigner?" And he said to him, "Arise, go your way; your faith has saved you."

And then the Pharisees demanded of him to know when the kingdom of God should come. He answered them and said, "The kingdom of God does not come with observation. Neither shall men say, 'Look here,' or 'Look there,' for behold, the kingdom of God is within you." And he said to the disciples, "The days will come, when you will desire to see one of the days of the Son of man, but you will not see it. Then they will say to you, 'Behold here,' or 'Behold there,' but do not go there, neither follow them. For like the lightning that flashes out of the one part of the sky and shines to the other part, so shall the Son of man be in his day. But first he must suffer many things and be rejected by this generation. And as it was in the days of Noah, so shall it be in the days of the Son of man. They ate, they drank, they married wives and gave in marriage, until the day that Noah went into the ark, and the flood came and destroyed them all. Likewise was it in the days of Lot: they ate, they drank, they bought, they sold, they planted, they built. But on the day that Lot went out from Sodom, it rained fire and brimstone from heaven and destroyed them all. Accordingly shall it be on the day when the Son of man will be revealed. On that day he that is on top of the house and his goods are in the house, he must not come down to get them. Likewise, he that is in the field, he must not turn back to what he left behind. Remember Lot's wife. Whoever seeks to keep his life will lose it, and whoever loses his life will keep it. I tell you, on that night there shall be two in one bed: one will be taken and the other will be left. Two women will be grinding together: one will be taken and the other will be left. Two will be in the field: one will be taken and the other will be left." And they answered and said to him, "Where, Lord?" And he said to them, "Wherever the body is, there shall the eagles be gathered together also."

And he also told them a parable, to teach them that they ought to always pray and not grow weary, saying, "There was a judge in a certain city, who neither feared God nor respected man. And there was a widow in that city which came to him and said, 'Give me justice against my adversary.' And for a long time he would not, but then he said to himself, 'Though I do not fear God nor respect man, yet because this widow troubles me I will give her justice; otherwise she will keep coming and make me weary.'" And the Lord said, "Hear what the unrighteous judge said. Will God not give justice to his elect, which cry to him day and night? Yes. And will he make them wait for long? I tell you he will give justice to them quickly. But when the Son of man comes, will he find faith on the earth?"

He also told this parable about those which think of themselves as being righteous, yet despise others. "Two men went up into the temple to pray; one was a Pharisee and the other a tax collector. The Pharisee stood and prayed thus to himself, 'O God, I thank you that I am not like other men: extortioners, unjust, adulterers, or even like this tax collector. I fast twice a week; I give a tithe on all that I receive.' But the tax collector, standing far away, would not so much as lift up his eyes to heaven, but struck his chest, saying, 'O God, be merciful to me a sinner.' I tell you, this man departed to his house justified, rather than the other. For every man that exalts himself shall be humbled, and he that humbles himself shall be exalted."

And they brought babies to him so that he would touch them. When his disciples saw it, they rebuked them. But Jesus called them to him and said, "Allow the children to come to me and do not forbid them, for of such is the kingdom of God. Truly I say to you, whoever does not receive the kingdom of God like a child will not enter in." Then a certain ruler asked him, saying, "Good Master, what should I do to inherit eternal life?" And Jesus said to him, "Why do you call me good? No one is good except God alone. You know the commandments: do not commit adultery, do not kill, do not steal, do not bear false witness, honor your father and your mother." And he said, "All of these I have kept from my youth." Now when Jesus heard that, he said to him, "Yet you lack one thing. Sell all that you have and give to the poor and you will have treasure in heaven, and come follow me." But when he heard those things he became very sad, because he had great wealth. And when Jesus saw him very sorrowful, he said, "With much difficulty shall those with riches enter into the kingdom of God! It is surely easier for a camel to go through the eye of a needle, than for a rich man to enter into the kingdom of God." Then those that heard it said, "Who then will be saved?" And he said, "The things which are impossible with men, are possible with God."

Then Peter said, "Look, we have left everything and have followed you." And he said to them, "Truly I say to you, there is no one that has left house, or parents, or brothers, or wife, or children for the sake of the kingdom of God, which will not receive much more in this world, and eternal life in the world to come."

Then Jesus took the twelve aside and said to them, "Behold, we are going up to Jerusalem, and all things shall be fulfilled about the Son of man that were written by the prophets. For he will be handed over to the Gentiles, and will be mocked and treated shamefully and spit upon. And after they have flogged him, they will put him to death; but on the third day he will rise again." But they did not understand these things and the words were hidden from them, neither did they comprehend what was said.

And it came to pass, as he came near to Jericho, that a certain blind man sat begging on the side of the road. And when he heard the crowds pass by, he asked what it meant, and they told him that Jesus of Nazareth had passed by. Then he cried out, saying, "Jesus the Son of David, have mercy on me." And the ones in the front rebuked him and told him to hold his peace, but he cried even more, "O Son of David, have mercy on me." And Jesus stopped and commanded that he be brought to him. And when he came near, he asked him, "What do you want me to do for you?" And he said, "Lord, allow me to receive my sight." And Jesus said to him, "Receive your sight; your faith has saved you." Immediately he received his sight and followed him, praising God. And when all the people saw this, they gave praise to God.

Now when Jesus entered and passed through Jericho, behold, a man named Zacchaeus was there, who was the chief tax collector and was rich. And he wanted to see who Jesus was, but could not because of the crowd and because he was a short man. Therefore he ran ahead and climbed up into a wild fig tree, so that he might see him, because he was coming that way. When Jesus came to the place, he looked up and saw him and said to him, "Zacchaeus, come down at once, because I must stay at your house today." Then he came down quickly and welcomed him joyfully. And when everyone saw it, they murmured, saying that he had gone in to be a guest with a sinful man. And Zacchaeus stood and said to the Lord, "Behold, Lord, half of my possessions I will give to the poor; and if I have taken from any man by false accusations, I will give back to him fourfold." Then Jesus said to him, "Today salvation has come to this house, since he also has become a son of Abraham. For the Son of man has come to seek and to save that which was lost." And while they listened to these things, he continued and told a parable because he was near to Jerusalem and also because they thought that the kingdom of God would soon appear. Therefore he said, "A certain noble man traveled to a far country to receive a kingdom for himself and then return. He called his ten servants and handed them ten pieces of silver and said to them, 'Conduct business until I return.' Now his citizens hated him and sent a delegation after him, saying, 'We will not have this man to rule over us.' And it came to pass, after he had received his kingdom and returned, that he commanded the servants to whom he had given the money to be called to him, that he might know what every man had earned. The first came and said, 'Lord, your piece has increased ten pieces.' And he said to him, 'Well done, good servant. Since you have been faithful in a very little thing, you will have authority over ten cities.' And the second came and said, 'Lord, your piece has increased five pieces.' And he said to him, 'You will also be ruler over five cities.' Then the other came and said, 'Lord, behold your piece, which I have laid up in a handkerchief. For I feared you, knowing you to be a shrewd man, taking up what you did not lay down and reaping what you did not sow.' Then he said to him, 'Out of your own mouth will I judge you, you evil servant. You knew that I was a shrewd man who takes up what I did not lay down and reaps what I did not sow. Why then did you not put my money into the bank, so that when I came I would have received it with interest?' And he said to them that stood nearby, 'Take from him the piece and give it to him that has ten pieces.' And they said to him, 'Lord, he already has ten pieces.' 'For I say to you, to all them that have it shall be given, and from him that has not, even what he has shall be taken from him. Moreover, those enemies of mine—which do not want me to reign over them—bring them here and kill them before me.'" And when he had finished speaking he went on ahead, going up to Jerusalem.

Jesus Enters Jerusalem

And it came to pass, when he was near Bethphage and Bethany, beside the mountain which is called the Mount of Olives, he sent out two of his disciples and said, "Go into the town which is ahead of you, and as soon as you come into it you will find a colt tied up on which a man has never sat. Untie him and bring him here. And if anyone asks you why you are untying him, say to them, 'Because the Lord needs him.'" So they that were sent went on ahead and found it just like he had said to them. And as they were untying the colt, the owners said to them, "Why are you untying the colt?" And they said, "The Lord needs him."

So they brought the colt to Jesus and threw their garments on him, and set Jesus upon him. And as he went, they were spreading their coats on the road. And when he had come near to going down the Mount of Olives, the entire crowd of the disciples began to rejoice and to praise God with loud voices for all the powerful works that they had seen, saying, "Blessed is the King that comes in the Name of the Lord! Peace in heaven and glory in the highest places!" Then some of the Pharisees in the crowd said to him, "Master, rebuke your disciples." But he answered and said to them, "I tell you, that if they should hold their peace, the stones would cry out."

And as he approached, he beheld the city and wept for it, saying, "If you had only known this day in the very least the things which make for peace! But now they are hidden from your eyes. For the days are coming upon you, when your enemies will dig a trench around you and surround you and close in on you from every side. They will crush you and your children to the ground, and they will not leave one stone on top of another inside you, because you did not recognize the time of your visitation."

He also went into the temple, and began to throw out those which were selling and buying there, saying to them, "It is written, 'my house is a house of prayer,' but you have made it a den of thieves." And he taught daily in the temple. The high priests and the scribes and the leaders of the people sought to destroy him, but they did not know how they might do it because all the people were hanging on every word they heard from him.

And it came to pass on one of those days—as he was teaching the people in the temple and preaching the Gospel—that the high priests and the scribes came to him with the elders and spoke to him, saying, "Tell us by what authority you are doing these things, and who is it that has given you this authority?" And he answered and said to them, "I will also ask you one thing. Tell me, was the baptism of John from heaven or from men?" And they discussed it among themselves, saying, "If we reply 'from heaven,' he will say, 'Why then did you not believe him?' But if we reply 'from men,' all the people will stone us, because they are convinced that John was a prophet." Therefore they answered that they did not know from where it was. Then Jesus said to them, "Neither will I tell you by what authority I do these things."

Then he began to tell this parable to the people: "A certain man planted a vineyard and rented it out to tenants and went into a foreign country for a long time. After a while, he sent a servant to the tenants to receive of the fruit of the vineyard, but the tenants beat him and sent him away with nothing. Again he sent another servant, and they beat him and mistreated him and sent him away with nothing. And he sent a third, and they wounded him and threw him out. Then the owner of the vineyard said, 'What should I do? I will send my beloved son, maybe they will honor him when they see him.' But when the tenants saw him, they discussed it among themselves and said, 'This one is the heir. Let us kill him so that the inheritance may be ours.' So they threw him out of the vineyard and killed him. What will the owner of the vineyard therefore do unto them? He will come and destroy those tenants, and will rent out his vineyard to others." But when they heard it, they said, "God forbid." And he looked at them and said, "What does it mean that is written:

'The stone that the builders refused is made the head of the corner'? Everyone that falls upon that stone will be broken, and on everyone that it falls will be ground to powder."

Then the high priests and the scribes went out to lay hands on him that very hour because they understood that he had spoken this parable against them, but they feared the people. They watched him and sent out spies, who pretended to be righteous, listening for words to accuse him and hand him over to the power and authority of the governor. And they asked him, saying, "Master, we know that you say and teach what is right, because you do not show partiality and truly teach the way of God. Is it lawful for us to give taxes to Caesar or not?" But having perceived their craftiness, he said to them, "Why do you tempt me? Show me a penny. Whose image and title is on it?" They answered and said, "Caesar's." Then he said to them, "Then give to Caesar the things which are Caesar's and to God those which are God's." And they could not find fault with his saying in front of the people, but they were amazed by his answer and held their peace.

Then came to him some of the Sadducees (which deny that there is any resurrection) and they questioned him, saying, "Master, Moses wrote to us that if any man's brother should die, having a wife and no children, then his brother should take his wife, and raise up children for his brother. Now there were seven brothers, and the first took a wife and died without children. And the second took the wife, and he died childless. Then the third took her, and so likewise that the seven all died and left no children. Last of all, the woman also died. Therefore at the resurrection, whose wife of them shall she be, because all seven had her as a wife?" Then Jesus answered and said to them, "The children of this world marry wives and are married. But they which shall be counted worthy to enjoy that world and the resurrection from the dead, neither marry wives, neither are married, because they can no longer die and so they are like the angels, and are the sons of God since they are the children of the resurrection. That the dead will rise again was showed by Moses beside the bush, when he said, 'The Lord is the God of Abraham, and the God of Isaac, and the God of Jacob.' He is not the God of the dead, but of the living because all live unto him." Then some of the scribes answered and said, "Master, you have spoken well." After that, they dared not ask him anything further.

Then he said to them, "How do they say that Christ is David's son? David himself said in the book of the Psalms, 'The Lord said to my Lord, sit at my right hand until I make your enemies your footstool.' Since David called him Lord, how is he then his son?" Then with all the people listening, he said to his disciples, "Beware of the scribes, which willingly wear long robes, and love greetings in the markets, and the highest seats in the synagogues, and the places of honor at the feasts. They devour the houses of widows, and for appearances they make long prayers. They will receive greater condemnation."

And as he watched, he saw the rich men throwing their gifts into the treasury. He also saw a certain poor widow throw in two mites. And he said, "I tell you the truth, this poor widow has thrown in more than all of them. For all of them, out of their surplus, have thrown in offerings to God, but she, out of her poverty, has thrown in everything she has."

Some began speaking about the temple, how it was adorned with beautiful stones and consecrated things, and he said, "Are these the things at which you are looking? The days will come when a stone will not be left upon another that will not be thrown down." Then they asked him, saying, "Master, when shall these things happen, and what sign will there be when these things will come to pass?" And he said, "Take heed so that you are not deceived, because many will come in my Name, saying, 'I am Christ, and the time is near.' Do not follow them. When you hear about wars and riots, do not be afraid;

these things must come first, but the end is not yet." Then he said to them, "Nation will rise against nation, and kingdom against kingdom; great earthquakes shall be in many places, and hunger, plagues, and terrors. There will be great signs in the heavens. But before all this, they will capture you and persecute you, handing you over to the synagogues and the prisons, bringing you before kings and rulers for my Name's sake. This will be your time to give a testimony. Secure it in your hearts to not prepare ahead of time what you will answer. I will give you the words and the wisdom, and your adversaries will not be able to stand or speak against it. Yes, you will be betrayed by your parents, and your brothers, and your family, and your friends, and some of you will be put to death. You will be hated by all men for my Name's sake. Yet not one hair on your heads will perish. By your endurance, you will gain your lives."

"When you see Jerusalem surrounded by soldiers, understand that her desolation is near. Then let those who are in Judea flee to the mountains, and let those who are inside the city depart, and let not those who are in the country enter in. For these are the days of vengeance to fulfill all things which have been written. Woe to those that are with child, and to those that are nursing in those days, because there will be great distress in this land and wrath over this people; they will fall on the edge of the sword, and will be taken captive into all nations; and Jerusalem shall be trampled underfoot by the Gentiles, until the times of the Gentiles are fulfilled. Then there will be signs in the sun, and in the moon, and in the stars; and on the earth there will be distress among the nations, confused by the roaring of the sea and the waters. Men's hearts will fail with fear and anticipation of those things which shall come on the world, because the powers of heaven will be shaken. And then they will see the Son of man coming on a cloud, with power and great glory. And when these things begin to happen, stand up and lift up your heads, because your redemption is drawing near."

And he told them a parable, "Behold, the fig tree and all trees. When their shoots come forth and you see them, you yourselves know that summer is near. Likewise, when you see these things come to pass, you know that the kingdom of God is near. Truly, I say to you that this generation will not pass, until all these things are done. Heaven and earth will pass away, but my words will not pass away. Guard yourselves, lest at any time your hearts become burdened by distractions and drunkenness and the cares of this life, and that day catches you unaware like a trap; it will come upon all those that dwell on the face of the whole earth. Watch therefore and pray continually, that you may be counted worthy to escape all these things that will come to pass, and that you may stand before the Son of man."

Now during the day he taught in the temple and at night he went out and stayed on the mountain, which is called the Mount of Olives. And all the people came in the morning to him, to hear him in the temple.

The Last Passover

Now the feast of unleavened bread was drawing near, which is called the Passover. And the high priests and scribes were seeking how they might kill him, because they feared the people. Then Satan entered into Judas, called Iscariot, who was one of the twelve. And he went and spoke with the high priests and captains, about how he might betray him to them. So they were glad and agreed to give him money. And he consented, and looked for an opportunity to betray him unto them when they were away from the people.

Then came the day of unleavened bread, when the Passover lamb must be sacrificed. And he sent Peter and John, saying, "Go and prepare the Passover for us that we may eat it." And they said to him, "Where do you want us to go to prepare it?" Then he said to them, "Behold, when you enter the city, a man will meet you carrying a pitcher of water. Follow him into the house that he enters and say to the head man of the house, 'The Master says to you, "Where is the room where I shall eat my Passover with my disciples?"' Then he will show you a large room upstairs that is furnished. Make it ready there." So they went and found it just as he had said to them, and prepared the Passover.

When the time had come, he sat down, and the twelve apostles with him. Then he said to them, "I have earnestly wanted to eat this Passover with you before I suffer. For I say to you that from now on, I will not eat of it again until it is fulfilled in the kingdom of God." And he took the cup and gave thanks and said, "Take this and divide it among you. I tell you, I will not drink of the fruit of the vine until the kingdom of God has come." And he took bread, and when he had given thanks, he broke it and gave to them, saying, "This is my body which is given for you; do this in remembrance of me." After supper, he likewise took the cup, saying, "This cup is the new testament in my blood, which is shed for you. But see, the hand of him that betrays me is with me at the table. The Son of man will surely go as it has been appointed, but woe to that man by whom he has been betrayed." Then they began disputing among themselves which of them it should be that should do that.

And there also arose a disagreement among them as to which of them was the greatest. But he said to them, "The kings of the Gentiles reign over them, and they that bear rule over them are called benefactors. But you shall not be so; let the greatest among you be as the least, and the leader as one that serves. For who is greater: he that sits at the table, or he that serves? Is it not he that sits at the table? And I am with you as one that serves, and you have continued with me in my trials. Therefore I will appoint a kingdom to you, as my Father has appointed one to me, so that you may eat and drink at the table in my kingdom, and sit on thrones and judge the twelve tribes of Israel."

And the Lord said, "Simon, Simon, behold, Satan has requested to sift you like wheat. But I have prayed for you, that your faith will not fail. Therefore when you have turned again, strengthen your brothers." And he said to him, "Lord, I am ready to go with you into prison and to death." But he said, "I tell you, Peter, the rooster will not crow today, before you have three times denied that you knew me."

And he said to them, "When I sent you out without bag, or money, or shoes, did you lack anything?" And they said, "Nothing." Then he said to them, "But now, he that has a bag let him take it, and likewise any money, and he that has none, let him sell his coat and buy a sword. For I say to you that yet the things which are written must be performed by me: 'With the wicked shall he be numbered.' Of a certainty, those things which are written of me shall be fulfilled." And they said, "Lord, behold, here are two swords." And he said to them, "It is enough."

Jesus is Arrested

And he came out, and went (as was his custom) to the Mount of Olives and his disciples followed with him. And when he came to the place, he said to them, "Pray, lest you enter into temptation." And he drew aside from them about a stone's throw and kneeled down and prayed, saying, "Father, if you will it, take this cup away from me. Nevertheless, let not my will, but yours be done." And there appeared an angel to him from heaven, comforting him. Being in agony, he prayed more earnestly, and his sweat was like drops of blood, trickling down to the ground. And he rose up from prayer and came to his disciples, and found them sleeping because they were grieved. And he said to them, "Why are you sleeping? Rise and pray, lest you enter into temptation."

While he was speaking, behold, a crowd came. One of the twelve—he that was called Judas—was leading them and he came near to Jesus to kiss him. And Jesus said to him, "Judas, are you betraying the Son of man with a kiss?" Now when they which were with him, saw what would follow, they said to him, "Lord, shall we strike with the sword?" And one of them struck a servant of the high priest, cutting off his right ear. Then Jesus answered and said, "Let them alone," and he touched his ear and healed him. Then Jesus said to the high priests, and captains of the temple, and the elders who had come to him, "Do you come out as unto a thief, with swords and staffs? When I was with you everyday in the temple, you did not stretch out your hands against me. But this hour and the power of darkness are yours."

Then they took him and led him, and brought him to the high priest's house. And Peter followed a far way off. When they had kindled a fire in the middle of the courtyard and sat down together, Peter also sat down among them. A certain woman saw him as he sat by the fire, and having recognized him, said, "This man was also with him." But he denied it, saying, "Woman, I know him not." And after a little while, another man saw him, and said, "You are also with them." But Peter said, "Man, I am not." And about an hour later, a certain other affirmed, saying, "Surely this man was with him, for he is also a Galilean." And Peter said, "Man, I do not know what you are talking about." And immediately, while he was still speaking, the rooster crowed. Then the Lord turned back and looked at Peter, and Peter remembered the saying of the Lord, how he had said to him, "Before the rooster crows, you will three times deny me." And Peter went out and wept bitterly.

And the men that held Jesus mocked him and beat him. When they had blindfolded him, they struck him on the face and asked him, saying, "Prophesy who it is that struck you." Many other things did they blasphemously speak against him. And as soon as it was morning, the elders of the people, the high priests, and the scribes came together, and led him into their council, saying, "Are you the Christ? Tell us." And he said to them, "If I tell you, you will not believe it. And if I also question you, you will not answer me, nor let me go. Hereafter shall the Son of man sit at the right hand of the power of God." Then they all said, "Then you are the Son of God?" And he said to them, "You say that I am." Then they said, "What need do we have of any further witness? We ourselves have heard it from his own mouth."

Then the whole crowd of them arose and led him to Pilate. And they began to accuse him, saying, "We have found this man corrupting the nation, forbidding them to pay taxes to Caesar, saying that he is Christ, a king." And Pilate asked him, saying, "Are you the King of the Jews?" And he answered him and said, "You say it." Then Pilate said to the high priests and to the people, "I find no guilt in this man." But they were all the more fierce, saying, "He stirs up the people, teaching throughout all Judea, beginning in Galilee even to this place." Now when Pilate heard of Galilee, he asked whether the man were a Galilean. When it was confirmed that he was of Herod's jurisdiction, he sent him to Herod, who was also in Jerusalem in those days. And when Herod saw Jesus, he was exceedingly glad. He had wanted to see him for a long time, because he had heard many things about him, and hoped to see some sign done by him. Then he questioned him of many things, but he answered him nothing. The high priests and the scribes also stood by and accused him vehemently. And Herod, with his soldiers, despised him and mocked him, and dressed him in white and sent him again to Pilate. Pilate and Herod became friends of each other that very day, before that they had been enemies one to another.

Then Pilate called together the high priests, the rulers, and the people and said to them, "You have brought this man to me as one that corrupts the people. Behold, I have examined him before you and have found no guilt in this man of the things of which you accuse him. No, not even Herod, because I sent you to him and look, he found nothing worthy of death to be done by him. Therefore, I will flog him and let him loose." (It was required of him to free one prisoner to them at the feast.) Then all the crowd cried at once, saying, "Away with him and deliver Barabbas to us." (He was in prison for insurrection and murder.) Then Pilate spoke to them again, wanting to let Jesus loose. But they cried, saying, "Crucify, crucify him." And he said to them a third time, "But what evil has he done? I find no cause of death in him. I will therefore flog him and let him loose." But they were insistent with loud voices and demanded to have him crucified, and the voices of them and of the high priests prevailed. So Pilate gave the sentence, that it should be as they demanded. And he released the man they were asking for who had been thrown into prison for insurrection and murder, and he delivered Jesus over to their will.

As they led him away, they seized Simon of Cyrene as he was coming out of the field, and on him they laid the cross, to carry it behind Jesus. And there followed him a great crowd of people and of women, and the women mourned and lamented him. But Jesus turned back to them and said, "Daughters of Jerusalem, do not weep for me, but weep for yourselves and for your children. For behold, the days will come when men will say, 'Blessed are the barren and the wombs that never gave birth and the breasts which never nursed.' Then they shall begin to say to the mountains, 'Fall on us,' and to the hills, 'Cover us.' For if they do these things when the tree is green, what will happen when it is dry?"

There were two others, which were criminals, led with him to be crucified. And when they had come to the place which is called Calvary, they crucified him there, along with the criminals—one on the right hand and the other on the left. Then Jesus said, "Father, forgive them, for they do not know what they are doing." And they divided his clothing and cast lots. And the people stood and watched, and with them the rulers mocked him, saying, "He saved others, let him save himself if he is the Christ, the Chosen of God." The soldiers also mocked him, and came and offered him vinegar, saying, "If you are the King of the Jews, save yourself." And an inscription was also written over him—in Greek, in Latin, and in Hebrew: THIS IS THE KING OF THE JEWS.

And one of the criminals which were hanged there insulted him, saying, "If you are the Christ, save yourself and us." But the other answered and rebuked him, saying, "Do you not fear God, since you are under the same condemnation? We are indeed here justly, for we are receiving the things worthy of what we have done, but this man has done nothing wrong." And he said to Jesus, "Lord, remember me, when you come into your kingdom." Then Jesus said to him, "Truly I say to you, today you shall be with me in Paradise."

And it was about the sixth hour and there was a darkness over all the land until the ninth hour. The sun was darkened and the veil of the temple was torn down the middle. And Jesus cried out with a loud voice and said, "Father, into your hands I commit my spirit." And when he had said this, he gave up the ghost. Now when the centurion saw what had happened, he glorified God, saying, "Surely this was a righteous man." And all the people that came together to see it happen, watched the things which were done and struck their chests and returned. And all his friends and the women that followed him from Galilee stood a far way off, watching everything.

There was a man named Joseph on the council who was a good and righteous man. He did not consent to the counsel and deed of the others. He was from Arimathea, a city of the Jews, and was also waiting for the kingdom of God. He went to Pilate and asked for the body of Jesus. He took it down and wrapped it in a linen cloth, laying it in a tomb cut out of the rock in which no man was yet buried. It was the day of preparation and the Sabbath was drawing near. The women that came with him from Galilee followed after and saw the tomb where his body was laid. They returned and prepared perfumes and oils and rested on the Sabbath day, according to the commandment.

The Resurrection of the Christ

Now the first day of the week, early in the morning, they came to the tomb with some other women and brought the perfumes which they had prepared. And they found the stone rolled away from the tomb. They went in, but did not find the body of the Lord Jesus. And it came to pass, as they were amazed by this, behold, two men suddenly stood by them in shining clothes, and they were afraid and bowed down their faces to the earth. The men said to them, "Why do you seek him that lives among the dead? He is not here, but has risen. Remember how he spoke to you, when he was yet in Galilee, saying that the Son of man must be delivered into the hands of sinful men, and be crucified, and the third day rise again?" And they remembered his words and returned from the tomb, and told all these things to the eleven and to all those who remained. Now it was Mary Magdalene, Joanna, Mary the mother of James, and the other women with them which told these things to the apostles. But their words seemed to them as nonsense and they did not believe them. Then Peter got up and ran to the tomb, and looked in and saw only the linen clothes, and he departed wondering to himself what had happened.

And behold, two of them went that same day to a town called Emmaus, about seven miles from Jerusalem. And they talked together of all these things which were done. And it came to pass, as they were talking and discussing together that Jesus himself drew near and walked with them, but their eyes were kept from recognizing him. And he said to them, "What are you talking about with one another as you walk that is making you sad?" And the one, named Cleopas, answered and said to him, "Are you only a stranger in Jerusalem, not knowing of the things which have come to pass there in these days?" And he said to them, "What things?" And they said to him, "Of Jesus of Nazareth, who was a prophet, mighty in deed and in word before God and all people. And how the high priests and our rulers delivered him to be condemned to death and have him crucified. But we had hoped that he was the One that would deliver Israel, and regarding all these things, today is the third day from when they were done. Yes, and some women among us were astonished when they earlier went to the tomb. When they did not find his body, they returned, saying that they had also seen a vision of angels who said that he was alive. Therefore some of them which were with us went to the tomb, and found it just as the women had said, but they did not see him."

Then he said to them, "O fools and slow of heart to believe all that the prophets have spoken! Was it not necessary for the Christ to have suffered these things, and to enter into his glory?" And he began at Moses and all the Prophets, and interpreted to them the things in all the Scriptures which were written about him. And they drew near to the town which they were walking to, and he made as though he would have gone farther. But they urged him, saying, "Stay with us, for it is almost night, and the day is nearly gone." So he went in to stay with them. And it came to pass, as he sat at the table with them that he took the bread, and blessed, and broke it, and gave it to them. Then their eyes were opened, and they recognized him, but he disappeared from them. And they said between themselves, "Did not our hearts burn within us while he talked with us on the road, and when he opened the Scriptures up to us?" And they got up the same hour and returned to Jerusalem. When they found the eleven gathered together and them that were with them, they said, "The Lord is risen indeed, and has appeared to Simon." Then they told what things had happened on the road, and how he was recognized by them in the breaking of bread.

And as they told these things, Jesus himself stood in the middle of them and said to them, "Peace to you." But they were startled and afraid, assuming that they had seen a spirit. Then he said to them, "Why are you frightened and why do doubts arise in your hearts? Behold my hands and my feet; it is I myself. Touch me, and see; a spirit does not have flesh and bones, like you see that I have." And when he had said this, he showed them his hands and feet. And while they still could not believe it and were overjoyed and amazed, he said to them, "Do you have any food here?" And they gave him a piece of a broiled fish and a honeycomb, and he took it and ate it before them. And he said to them, "These are the words which I spoke to you while I was yet with you, that all must be fulfilled which are written about me in the Law of Moses, and in the Prophets, and in the Psalms. Then he opened their minds, that they might understand the Scriptures, and said to them, "Thus is it written, and thus it must be that the Christ should suffer, and rise again from the dead on the third day; and that repentance and the remission of sins shall be preached in his Name among all the nations, beginning at Jerusalem. Now you are witnesses of these things. Behold, I send the promise of my Father upon you; but wait in the city of Jerusalem, until you are clothed with power from on high." Afterward he led them out to Bethany, and lifted up his hands and blessed them. And it came to pass, that as he blessed them, he departed from them, and was carried up into heaven. And they worshiped him, and returned to Jerusalem with great joy, and they were continually in the temple, praising and blessing God. *Amen.*

Part Two

The Acts of the Apostles

In my first account, O Theophilus, I wrote of all that Jesus began to do and teach until the day when he was taken up, after he had, through the holy Ghost, given commandments to the apostles whom he had chosen. To them he also presented himself alive after he had suffered, by many unmistakable proofs, being seen by them over the span of forty days, and speaking of those things which pertained to the kingdom of God. And when he had gathered them together, he commanded them to not depart from Jerusalem, but to wait for the promise of the Father, which he said, "You have heard about from me. John indeed baptized with water, but you will be baptized with the holy Ghost within a few days."

Therefore, when they came together they asked him, saying, "Lord, will you at this time restore the kingdom to Israel?" And he said to them, "It is not for you to know the times or the seasons which the Father has placed by his own power. But you will receive power from the holy Ghost when he comes upon you, and you shall be my witnesses, both in Jerusalem and all of Judea, and in Samaria and to the ends of the earth." And when he had spoken these things and while they watched, he was lifted up and a cloud took him out of their sight. And while they looked steadfastly toward heaven as he went up, behold, two men stood next to them in white clothing. They said, "Men of Galilee, why do you stand here staring into heaven? This Jesus, who was taken up from you into heaven, shall likewise come, as you have watched him go into heaven."

Then they returned to Jerusalem from the mountain that is called the Mount of Olives—which is near Jerusalem—being a Sabbath day's journey away. And when they had come in, they went up to an upstairs room, where they were staying. Peter and James, John and Andrew, Philip and Thomas, Bartholomew and Matthew, James the son of Alphaeus and Simon the zealous one, and Judas James' brother all continued with one mind in prayer and supplication, together with the women and Mary the mother of Jesus and his brothers.

During those days, Peter stood up in the middle of the disciples—the number of which being in the place was about a hundred and twenty—and said: "Men and brothers, the Scripture was fulfilled which the holy Ghost spoke by the mouth of David regarding Judas, who was the guide for them that took Jesus. He was counted as one of us, and he received his share in this ministry. Therefore he purchased a field with the reward of his sin and when he had thrown himself down headfirst, he split apart and all his insides gushed out. And it is known to all the inhabitants of Jerusalem, insomuch that the field is called, 'Akel Dama' in their own language, which means, 'the field of blood.' For it is written in the book of Psalms, 'Let his home be desolate and let no man live there.' Also, 'Let another take his position.' Therefore of these men which have been with us all the time that the Lord Jesus was among us—beginning with the baptism of John to the day that he was lifted up from us—one of them must be made a witness with us of his resurrection."

And they presented two: Joseph called Barsabas (who was also called Justus) and Matthias. And they prayed, saying, "You, Lord, which know the hearts of all men, show which of these two you have chosen, that he may take the place of ministry and apostleship which Judas rejected to go to his own place." Then they cast their lots and the lot fell on Matthias, and it was agreed that he be counted with the eleven apostles.

The Day of Pentecost

And when the day of Pentecost had come, they were all with one mind in one place, when suddenly there came a sound from heaven, as of a gusting and mighty wind, and it filled the entire house where they sat. And there appeared to them divided tongues, like fire, and it sat upon each of them. And they were all filled with the holy Ghost and began to speak in other languages, as the Spirit gave them to speak.

And there were Jews living in Jerusalem, men that feared God from every nation under heaven. Now when this was heard, the crowd came together and was astonished, because every man heard them speaking in his own language. And they were amazed and marveled, saying among themselves, "Behold, are not these which are speaking all from Galilee? How then do we hear every man in our own language, from where we were born? Parthians and Medes, Elamites and the inhabitants of Mesopotamia, Judea and of Cappadocia, Pontus and Asia, Phrygia and Pamphylia, Egypt and of the parts of Libya which is beside Cyrene, strangers of Rome, Jews and converts, Cretans and Arabians—we hear them speak in our own language the wonderful works of God. They were all amazed and doubted, saying to each other, "What does this mean?" Others mocked and said, "They are full of new wine."

But Peter, standing with the eleven, raised his voice and said to them, "You men of Judea, and all of you that live in Jerusalem, understand this and listen to my words. They are not drunk, like you suppose, since it is only the third hour of the day. But this is what was spoken by the prophet Joel: 'It shall be in the last days, says God, that I will pour out my Spirit upon all flesh, and your sons and your daughters shall prophesy, and your young men shall see visions, and your old men shall dream dreams. And on my servants, both men and women, I will pour out my Spirit in those days, and they shall prophesy. And I will show wonders in heaven above, and signs in the earth beneath—blood and fire, and the vapors of smoke. The Sun shall be turned into darkness and the moon into blood, before the great and magnificent day of the Lord comes. And it shall be that whoever calls on the Name of the Lord shall be saved.'"

"Men of Israel, hear these words: Jesus of Nazareth, a man approved by God among you with great works and wonders and signs, which God did by him in your presence, as you yourselves also know, I tell you that he was delivered over by the designated plan and foreknowledge of God, after which you took him with wicked hands to be crucified and killed. But God raised him up, breaking the sorrow of death, because it was impossible that he should be held by it. For David said concerning him, 'I beheld the Lord always before me; he is at my right hand and I should not be shaken. Therefore my heart rejoiced and my tongue was glad. Moreover my flesh will rest in hope, because you will not leave my soul in the grave; neither allow your holy One to see corruption. You have shown me the ways of life, and shall make me full of joy with your presence.'"

"Men and brothers, I speak boldly to you about the patriarch David; he is both dead and buried and his tomb remains with us to this day. Therefore, since he was a prophet, he knew that God had sworn an oath to him: He would raise up the Christ from among his descendants, according to the flesh, and set him upon his throne. Knowing this beforehand, he spoke of the resurrection of the Christ—that his soul would not be left in the grave, neither would his flesh see corruption. This Jesus God has raised up, of which we are all witnesses. Since he has been exalted to the right hand of God, and has received from his Father the promise of the holy Ghost, he has brought forth this which you now see and hear. For David has not ascended into heaven, but he said, 'The Lord said to my Lord, sit at my right hand until I make your enemies your footstool.' Therefore, let all the house of Israel know for certain that God has made him both Lord and Christ, this Jesus whom you crucified."

Now when they heard it, they were pierced in their hearts and said to Peter and the other apostles, "Men and brothers, what shall we do?" Then Peter said to them, "Repent and be baptized, every one of you in the Name of Jesus Christ for the remission of sins and you will receive the gift of the holy Ghost. The promise is made to you, and to your children, and to all that are far off, as many as the Lord our God shall call." And with many other words he testified and exhorted them, saying, "Save yourselves from this corrupt generation."

Then those which gladly received his word were baptized, and that same day there were about three thousand souls added to the Church. And they devoted themselves to the apostles' teaching and fellowship, the breaking of bread, and prayers. And fear came upon every soul and many wonders and signs were being done by the apostles. All that believed were together in one place and had all things in common. They sold their possessions and goods and shared them with all men, as anyone had need. And they continued daily with one mind in the temple; breaking bread at home and eating their meals together with gladness and unity of heart, praising God and having favor with all the people. And the Lord was adding to the Church each day with those who were being saved.

Peter and John

Now Peter and John went up together into the temple at the ninth hour of prayer, and a certain man which was crippled from his mother's womb was carried and laid daily at the gate of the temple called Beautiful, to ask for charity from those that entered in. Seeing Peter and John about to enter into the temple, he asked them for charity. And Peter earnestly looking at him with John, said, "Look at us." And he looked at them, hoping to receive something from them. Then Peter said, "I have no silver or gold, but what I do have, I will give to you. In the Name of Jesus Christ of Nazareth, stand up and walk." And he took him by the right hand and helped him up, and immediately his feet and ankle bones received strength. And he jumped up, stood and walked, and entered into the temple with them, walking and leaping and praising God. And all the people saw him walking, and praised God. They recognized him as the one which sat for charity at the Beautiful gate of the Temple, and they were amazed and astonished at what had happened to him.

And as the cripple who was healed held on to Peter and John, all the people were amazed and ran to them on the porch which is called Solomon's. When Peter saw it, he said to the people, "Men of Israel, why are you amazed by this? Why do you stare at us, as though by our own power or godliness we have healed this man? The God of Abraham and Isaac and Jacob, the God of our fathers has glorified his Son, Jesus, whom you betrayed and denied in front of Pilate, after he had determined to release him. But you denied the holy and righteous One, desiring that a murderer be given to you, and killed the Lord of life, whom God has raised from the dead—of which we are witnesses. And his Name has healed this man, whom you see and know. Through faith in his Name—and the faith which is given by him—he has given to him this perfect health of his whole body in the presence of you all."

"Brothers, I know that it was through ignorance that you did it, as your governors did also. But those things, which God had beforehand told by the words of all his prophets—that the Christ should suffer—he has thus fulfilled. Repent therefore and return, that your sins may be forgiven and the times of refreshing shall come from the presence of the Lord. And he will send Jesus Christ, who was before preached to you, whom the heaven must retain until the time when all things will be restored, which God has spoken through the words of all his holy prophets since the world began. Moses said to the fathers, 'The Lord your God will raise up for you a Prophet like me from out of your brothers; you shall listen to him in everything he says to you. It shall be that every person which shall not hear that Prophet, shall be destroyed out of the people.' Likewise, all the prophets from Samuel onward who have spoken have foretold of these days. You are the children of the prophets and of the covenant which God has made to our fathers, saying to Abraham, 'Even in your seed shall all the families of the earth be blessed.' For you first has God raised up his Son Jesus, and sent him to bless you by turning everyone of you from your sins."

As they were speaking to the people, the priests and the captain of the temple and the Sadducees came up to them, annoyed that they were teaching the people and preaching the resurrection from the dead in Jesus' Name. And they arrested them and held them in custody until the next day, because it was now evening. Even so, many of them which heard the word believed, and the number of the men was about five thousand.

It came to pass the next day that the rulers and elders and scribes were gathered together in Jerusalem, as were Annas the chief priest and Caiaphas and John and Alexander, and as many as were of the family of the high priest. And when they had set them before them, they asked, "By what power or in what Name have you done this?" Then Peter, full of the holy Ghost, said to them, "You rulers of the people and elders of Israel, if we are being examined this day because of the good deed done to the crippled man and by what means he is made well, be it known to all of you and to all the people of Israel, that by the Name of Jesus Christ of Nazareth, whom you crucified and whom God raised again from the dead, it is by him that this man stands healed before you. This is the stone which you builders threw aside which has become the head of the corner. Neither is there salvation in any other because there is given no other Name under heaven among men by which we must be saved."

When they saw the boldness of Peter and John and recognized that they were uneducated and untrained men, they were amazed, and knew they had been with Jesus. They also looked at the man who was healed standing with them and they had nothing to say against it. Then they commanded them to go aside out of the council and discussed among themselves, saying, "What shall we do to these men? Surely a public sign has been done by them and it is openly known to everyone that dwells in Jerusalem, we cannot deny it. But that it be told no more among the people, let us threaten and warn them that from now on they may no longer speak to anyone in this Name." So they called for them and commanded that they could not speak nor teach in the Name of Jesus at all. But Peter and John answered them and said, "Whether it is right in the sight of God to obey you rather than God, judge for yourselves, because we cannot help but to speak about the things which we have seen and heard." So they threatened them and let them go, finding nothing to punish them with and because of the people. All men praised God for what had been done, because the man was over forty years old on whom this miracle of healing was performed.

As soon as they were let go, they went to their friends and reported all that the high priests and elders had said to them. When they heard it, they lifted up their voices to God with one accord and said, "O Lord, you are the God which had made the heaven, the earth, the sea, and everything that is in them. By the mouth of your servant David you have said, 'Why do the Gentiles rage and the people imagine futile things? The kings of the earth gathered and the rulers came together against the Lord and against his Christ.' For doubtless, against your holy Son Jesus, whom you have anointed, have both Herod and Pontius Pilate—along with the Gentiles and the people of Israel—gathered themselves together to do whatever your hand and your counsel had determined beforehand to be done. And now, O Lord, behold their threats and grant to your servants to speak your word with boldness, and that you will stretch out your hand so that healings, signs, and wonders may be done in the Name of your holy Son Jesus." And when they had prayed, the place was shaken where they were gathered together, and they were all filled with the holy Ghost, and they spoke the word of God boldly.

And all of them that believed were of one heart and of one soul; neither did any of them say that anything which he possessed was his own, but they had all things in common. And the apostles bore witness to the resurrection of the Lord Jesus with great power, and great grace was upon them all. Neither was there any among them that lacked, because those who owned land or houses sold them and brought the money from the things that were sold and laid it down at the apostles' feet, and it was distributed unto every man, according to his needs. Joseph, called Barnabas by the apostles (which translated means "the son of encouragement"), being a Levite from the country of Cyprus, had land which he sold, and he brought the money and laid it down at the apostles' feet.

However, a certain man named Ananias and his wife Sapphira sold a possession and kept some of the money, his wife also being in agreement, bringing only a portion and laying it down at the apostles' feet. Then Peter said, "Ananias, why has Satan filled your heart, that you would lie to the holy Ghost by keeping part of the price of this possession? While it remained unsold, did it not belong to you? And after it was sold, was it not in your own power? Why then have you conceived this thing in your heart? You have not lied to men, but to God." When Ananias heard these words, he fell down and breathed his last. Then great fear came on all of them that heard these things. And the young men stood and lifted him up, and carried him out and buried him.

And it came to pass about three hours later that his wife came in, not knowing about what had happened. And Peter said to her, "Tell me, did you sell the land for so much?" And she said, "Yes, for so much." Then Peter said to her, "Why have you agreed together to tempt the Spirit of the Lord? Look, the feet of them which have buried your husband are at the door, and they shall carry you out." Then she immediately fell down at his feet, and breathed her last; and the young men came in and found her dead, and carried her out and buried her by her husband. And great fear came on all the church, and on all that heard these things.

Thus by the hands of the apostles were many signs and wonders done before the people, and they were all with one accord in Solomon's porch. And of the others no man dared to join them; nevertheless the people magnified them, and the number of them that believed in the Lord, both of men and women, grew more and more. And they would bring the sick into the streets, laying them on beds and couches so that when Peter walked by that at least his shadow might fall on them. There also came a crowd out of the cities around Jerusalem bringing the sick and those afflicted with unclean spirits, and they were all healed.

Then the chief priest rose up, and all those that were with him (which was the sect of the Sadducees), full of indignation. They laid hands on the apostles and put them in the common prison. But during the night, the angel of the Lord opened the prison doors and brought them out and said, "Go your way and stand in the temple, and speak all the words of life to the people. When they heard it, they entered into the temple early in the morning and taught. And the chief priest came and those that were with him, and called the council and all the elders of the children of Israel together, and sent to the prison to have them brought out. But when the officers came and did not find them in the prison, they returned and told it, saying, "Certainly we found the prison shut as tight as possible, and the keepers standing outside in front of the doors, but when we opened it we found no one inside."

When the chief priest and the captain of the temple and the high priests heard this, they doubted and wondered what this meant. Then one came in and told them, saying, "Behold, the men that you put in prison are standing in the temple and teaching the people." Then the captain with the officers went and brought them in without violence (for they feared the people, lest they should be stoned). And when they had brought them in, they stood before the council and the chief priest asked them, saying, "Did we not strictly command you that you should not teach in this Name? And now you have filled Jerusalem with your doctrine, bringing this man's blood upon us." Then Peter and the apostles answered and said, "We must obey God rather than men. The God of our fathers has raised up Jesus, whom you killed and hanged on a tree. God has lifted him up with his right hand to be a Prince and a Savior, to give repentance to Israel and forgiveness of sins. And we are his witnesses concerning these things which we proclaim, yes, and the holy Ghost, whom God has given to those that obey him."

Now when they heard this, they became enraged and wanted to kill them. Then a certain Pharisee of the council, named Gamaliel—a teacher of the Law and honored of all the people—stood up and commanded that the apostles be placed outside for a little while. Then he said to them, "Men of Israel, be careful about what you intend to do regarding these men. Before these days, Theudas rose up and boasted of himself, and a group of about four hundred men gathered around him. He was slain and all of them which obeyed him were scattered and brought to nothing. After this man, Judas of Galilee rose up during the days of the census, and drew many people after him. He also perished, and all that obeyed him were scattered abroad. Now I say to you to refrain yourselves from these men, and let them alone. If their plan or their work is of men, it will come to nothing; but if it is of God, you will not destroy it, because you will find yourselves fighting against God." And they agreed with him and called the apostles; and after they had beaten them they commanded that they should not speak in the Name of Jesus and let them go. So they departed from the Council, rejoicing that they were counted worthy to suffer for his Name. And daily in the temple and from house to house, they did not cease teaching and preaching Jesus Christ.

The Murder of Stephen

And in those days, as the number of the disciples grew, there arose a complaint from the Hellenists against the Hebrews, because their widows were being neglected in the daily ministering. Then the twelve called all of the disciples together and said, "It is not good for us to leave the word of God to serve the tables. Therefore brothers, find seven men among you of honest report and full of the holy Ghost and wisdom, which we may appoint to do this business. Then we can give ourselves continually to prayer and to the ministry of the word." And the saying pleased them all and they chose Stephen—a man full of faith and of the holy Ghost—and Philip, and Prochorus, and Nicanor, and Timon, and Parmenas, and Nicolas—a convert from Antioch. They stood them before the apostles, and they prayed and laid their hands on them. And the word of God increased, and the number of the disciples multiplied greatly in Jerusalem, and a great many of the priests were becoming obedient to the faith.

Now Stephen was full of faith and power and did great wonders and miracles among the people. Then there arose some from what was called the Synagogue of the Libertines—from Cyrenia and

Alexandria, and from Cilicia and Asia—and argued with Stephen. Since they were not able to resist the wisdom and the Spirit by which he spoke, they instigated men to say, "We have heard him speak blasphemous words against Moses and God." Thus they stirred up the people and the elders and the scribes, and running toward him, they caught him and brought him to the council. They also brought forth false witnesses which said, "This man does not stop speaking blasphemous words against this holy place and the Law. We have heard him say that this Jesus of Nazareth will destroy this place, and change the customs which Moses gave to us." And as all that sat on the Council looked at him steadfastly, they saw his face was like the face of an angel.

Then the chief priest said, "Are these things so?" And he said, "Men, brothers, and fathers, hear me. The God of glory appeared to our father Abraham while he was in Mesopotamia, before he dwelt in Haran, and said to him, 'Come out of your country and away from your kindred, and come into the land which I will show you.' Then he came out of the land of the Chaldeans and dwelt in Haran. And after his father had died, God brought him from there into this land, where you are now living, but he gave him no inheritance in it—not even a foot of the ground—yet he promised that he would give it to him for a possession and to his seed after him, even though he had no child. But God promised that his descendants would be sojourners in a strange land and that they would be kept in bondage and mistreated for four hundred years. 'But the nation to whom they shall be in bondage, I will judge,' God said, 'and after that they will come forth and serve me in this place.' He also gave him the covenant of circumcision, and to Abraham was born Isaac and he was circumcised the eighth day. To Isaac was born Jacob, and to Jacob the twelve patriarchs. And the patriarchs became envious and sold Joseph into Egypt, but God was with him and delivered him out of all his afflictions. He gave him favor and wisdom in the sight of Pharaoh, king of Egypt, who made him governor over Egypt and over his whole house."

"Then there was a famine over all the land of Egypt and Canaan, and great affliction, such that our fathers found no food. When Jacob heard that there was corn in Egypt, he sent our fathers first. And the second time, Joseph was recognized by his brothers and Joseph's family was made known to Pharaoh. Then Joseph sent and called for his father to be brought, and all his family, seventy-five souls in all. So Jacob went down into Egypt and he died, he and our fathers. They were taken into Shechem and were put into the tomb that Abraham had bought for silver from the sons of Hamor, son of Shechem."

"But when the time of the promise which God had sworn to Abraham drew near, the people grew and multiplied in Egypt until another king arose, one which did not know Joseph. He dealt treacherously with our people and oppressed our fathers, and made them throw out their young children, that they should not remain alive. At this time, Moses was born and was acceptable to God and was raised up in his father's house for three months. When he was thrown out, Pharaoh's daughter took him and raised him as her own son. And Moses was educated in all the wisdom of the Egyptians, and he was mighty in words and in deeds. When he was forty years old, it came into his heart to visit his brethren, the children of Israel. And when he saw one of them being mistreated, he defended him, avenging the mistreated by striking down the Egyptian. He supposed that his brethren would have understood that God was giving them deliverance by his hand, but they did not understand it. The next day, he showed himself to them as they fought with each other. Wanting to set them at peace again, he said, 'Men, you are brothers, why do you do wrong to one another?' But he that did his neighbor wrong pushed him away and said, 'Who made you a prince and a judge over us? Are you going to kill me, as you did the Egyptian yesterday?' When he heard this, Moses fled and became an exile in the land of Midian, where two sons were born to him."

"When forty years had passed, an angel of the Lord appeared to him in the wilderness of Mount Sinai, within a flame of fire in a bush. When Moses saw it he was amazed at the sight, and as he moved to observe it more closely, the voice of the Lord came to him, saying, 'I am the God of your fathers: the God of Abraham, and the God of Isaac, and the God of Jacob.' Then Moses trembled and did not dare to look. Then the Lord said to him, 'Remove the shoes from your feet because the place where you are standing is holy ground. I have surely seen the oppression of my people in Egypt, and I have heard their groaning, and I have come down to deliver them. Now come, and I will send you into Egypt.' This Moses, whom they forsook by saying, 'Who made you a prince and a judge?' was sent by God as a prince and a deliverer by the hand of the angel which appeared to him in the bush. He brought them out, showing signs and miracles in the land of Egypt and in the Red Sea and in the wilderness for forty years. This is that Moses which said to the children of Israel, 'A Prophet shall the Lord your God raise up for you from out of your brethren, just as I was, and to him shall you listen.' This is the one who was in the congregation in the wilderness with the angel, who spoke to him on Mount Sinai, and with our fathers. The one whom received the living oracles to give to us and to whom our fathers refused to obey, turning back again to Egypt in their hearts and saying to Aaron, 'Make us gods to lead us, because we do not know what has become of this Moses that brought us out of the land of Egypt.' And they made a calf in those days and offered sacrifice to the idol, and rejoiced in the works of their own hands. Then God turned himself away, and gave them up to serve the host of heaven, as it is written in the book of the Prophets, 'O house of Israel, have you offered slain beasts and sacrifices to me for forty years in the wilderness? You took up the tabernacle of Moloch and the star of your god Remphan, the images which you made to worship; therefore I will carry you away beyond Babylon.'"

"Our fathers had the tabernacle of witness in the wilderness, as he had appointed when he spoke to Moses saying that he should make it according to the pattern that he had seen. This tabernacle also our fathers received, and brought it in with Joshua when they defeated the nations which God drove out from before them, until the days of David. He found favor with God and desired that he might find a dwelling for the God of Jacob, but Solomon built him a house. However the most High does not dwell in temples made with hands, as the prophet says, 'Heaven is my throne, and earth is my footstool; what house will you build for me, says the Lord? What place should I rest in? Has not my own hand made all these things?' You men who are stiff-necked and uncircumcised in your hearts and ears, you have always resisted the holy Ghost; just as your fathers did, so do you. Which of the prophets have your fathers not persecuted? They killed those which were announcing the coming of the righteous One, of whom you are now the betrayers and murderers; you who have received the law as if delivered by angels, yet have not kept it."

When they heard these things, they became enraged and gnashed at him with their teeth. Being full of the holy Ghost, he looked intently into heaven and saw the glory of God and Jesus standing at the right hand of God. He said, "Behold, I see the heavens open and the Son of man standing at the right hand of God." Then they gave a shout with a loud voice and covered their ears, and rushed at him violently all at once. They drove him out of the city and stoned him, and the witnesses laid down their garments at the feet of a young man named Saul. And they stoned Stephen, who called on God and said, "Lord Jesus receive my spirit." And he kneeled down and cried with a loud voice, "Lord, do not hold this sin against them." And when he had thus spoken, he slept; and Saul consented to his death.

At that time, there was a great persecution against the Church in Jerusalem, and they were all scattered abroad, throughout the regions of Judea and Samaria, all except the apostles. Then certain God-fearing men carried Stephen among them to be buried, weeping loudly for him. But Saul began ravaging the Church, entering into every house and drawing out both men and women and putting them into prison. Therefore those that were scattered abroad went everywhere preaching the word.

Philip came to the city of Samaria and preached Christ to them. And the people listened to the things which Philip spoke with one mind, hearing and seeing the miracles which he did. Unclean spirits, crying with a loud voice, came out of many that were possessed of them; and many which were paralyzed or lame were being healed. There was great joy in that city. There was a certain man in the city called Simon, who used witchcraft and astonished the people of Samaria, claiming that he was some great man. They paid attention to him, from the least to the greatest, saying, "This man has a great power from God." And they listened to him because for a long time he had amazed them with sorcery. But as soon as they believed Philip, who preached of the things concerning the kingdom of God and the Name of Jesus Christ, they were baptized, both men and women. Then Simon himself also believed and was baptized and continued on with Philip. When he saw the signs and great miracles which were being done, he was amazed.

Now when the apostles, who were in Jerusalem, heard it said that Samaria had received the word of God, they sent Peter and John to them. And when they had come down to them, they prayed that they might receive the holy Ghost, because he had not yet come down on them and they had been baptized only in the Name of the Lord Jesus.

Then they laid their hands on them and they received the holy Ghost. When Simon saw that the holy Ghost was given through the apostles' laying on of hands, he offered them money and said, "Give this power to me also, that on whomsoever I lay hands, he may receive the holy Ghost." Then Peter said to him, "May your money perish with you, because you think that you can obtain the gift of God with money. You have neither part nor portion in this matter because your heart is not right in the sight of God. Therefore repent of your wickedness and pray to God that, if possible, the thoughts of your heart may be forgiven, because I perceive that you are poisoned by bitterness and held captive by iniquity." Then Simon answered and said, "Pray to the Lord for me, that none of these things which you have spoken may come upon me. When they had testified and preached the word of the Lord, they returned to Jerusalem, preaching the Gospel in many towns of the Samaritans.

Then the angel of the Lord spoke to Philip, saying, "Arise, and go toward the south on the road that goes down from Jerusalem to Gaza, where it is desert." So he got up and went. And behold, a certain eunuch from Ethiopia, an official for Candace, the queen of the Ethiopians, who was in charge of all her treasure, had come to Jerusalem to worship. As he returned sitting in his chariot, he was reading Isaiah the prophet. Then the Spirit said to Philip, "Go near and join yourself with this chariot." And Philip ran there, and heard him reading the prophet Isaiah. He said, "Do you understand what you are reading?" And he said, "How can I, unless someone guides me?" And he asked Philip to come up and sit with him. Now the part of the Scripture which he was reading was this: "He was led like a sheep to the slaughter, and like a lamb was silent before his shearer, so he does not open his mouth. In his humiliation his judgment has been lifted up, but who shall declare his generation, because his life is taken from the earth?" Then the Eunuch replied to Philip and said,

"I ask you, of whom is the prophet speaking? Of himself or of some other man?" Then Philip opened his mouth, and beginning with the same Scripture, he preached Jesus unto him. And as they were travelling on the road, they came to some water, and the Eunuch said, "Look, here is water; what prevents me from being baptized?" And Philip said to him, "If you believe with all your heart, you may." Then he answered and said, "I believe that Jesus Christ is the Son of God." Then he commanded the chariot to stop, and they went down into the water, both Philip and the Eunuch, and he baptized him. And as soon as they had come up out of the water, the Spirit of the Lord caught Philip away and the Eunuch saw him no more, and he went on his way rejoicing. But Philip was found in Azotus, and he walked everywhere preaching in all the cities until he came to Caesarea.

Saul Meets the Christ

Then Saul, still breathing out threats and murder against the disciples of the Lord, went to the high priest, and asked him for letters to the synagogues of Damascus, that if he found any men or women that were of the Way, he might bring them captive to Jerusalem. As he journeyed, it happened that as he came near to Damascus, there shined suddenly around him a light from heaven. He fell to the earth and heard a voice saying to him, "Saul, Saul, why are you persecuting me?" And he said, "Who are you, Lord?" And the Lord said, "I am Jesus whom you are persecuting; it is hard for you to kick against the prods." Then he was both trembling and astonished and said, "Lord, what do you want me to do?" And the Lord said to him, "Get up and go into the city and it shall be told to you what you shall do." The men who journeyed with him stood amazed, hearing a voice but seeing no man. And Saul got up from the ground and opened his eyes, but saw no one. Then they led him by the hand and brought him into Damascus. He was there for three days without sight and neither ate nor drank.

There was a certain disciple in Damascus named Ananias, and the Lord said to him in a vision, “Ananias.” And he said, “Behold, I am here, Lord.” Then the Lord said to him, “Get up and go into the street which is called Straight, and look in the house of Judas for a man called Saul of Tarsus. Behold, he is praying and has seen in a vision a man named Ananias coming in to him and putting his hands on him, so that he may regain his sight.” Then Ananias answered, “Lord, I have heard from many about this man, how he has done much evil to your saints in Jerusalem. Moreover, he is here on the authority of the high priests, to bind all that call on your Name.” Then the Lord said to him, “Go your way, for he is a chosen vessel unto me, to bear my Name before the Gentiles and kings and the children of Israel. I will show him how many things he must suffer for my Name’s sake.”

Then Ananias went his way and entered into that house, and put his hands on him and said, “Brother Saul, the Lord Jesus that appeared to you on the road as you were coming has sent me, that you may regain your sight and be filled with the holy Ghost.” And immediately there fell from his eyes something like scales and he regained his sight, and got up and was baptized. Then he ate some food and was strengthened. So Saul stayed with the disciples in Damascus for several days. And he immediately began preaching Christ in the synagogues, that he was the Son of God. And all that heard him were amazed and said, “Is this not the man who was ravaging them which called on this Name in Jerusalem and came here with that intent, that he should bring them bound to the high priests?” But Saul increased in strength and confounded the Jews living in Damascus, proving that Jesus was the Christ.

After many days had went by, the Jews conspired to kill him, but their plot was made known to Saul. They kept watch on the gates day and night so that they might kill him, but the disciples took him at night and put him through the wall and lowered him down in a basket by a rope. When Saul arrived in Jerusalem, he attempted to join himself with the disciples, but they were all afraid of him and did not believe that he was a disciple. Then Barnabas took him and brought him to the apostles and declared to them how he had seen the Lord on the road and that he had spoken to him, and how he had spoken boldly in Damascus in the Name of Jesus. So he joined with them at Jerusalem and spoke boldly in the Name of the Lord Jesus. He spoke and disputed with the Hellenists, but they were trying to kill him. When the brethren found out about it, they brought him to Caesarea and sent him off to Tarsus. Then the churches throughout all Judea and Galilee and Samaria had peace and were edified, going forth in the fear of the Lord and being multiplied by the comfort of the holy Ghost.

Peter's Vision

It came to pass as Peter was walking everywhere that he came also to the saints which lived in Lydda. He found a certain man there named Aeneas, who had been bedridden and paralyzed for eight years. Peter said to him, "Aeneas, Jesus Christ has made you whole. Get up and make your bed." And he immediately stood up. Everyone that lived in Lydda and Sharon saw him and turned to the Lord. There was also a certain woman in Joppa, a disciple named Tabitha (which is translated as Dorcas). She was full of good works and acts of mercy. And it happened in those days that she became sick and died; and after they had washed her, they laid her in an upstairs room. Since Lydda was close to Joppa and the disciples had heard that Peter was there, they sent two men to him, asking that he would come to them without delay. Then Peter got up and went with them and when he had arrived, they brought him to the upstairs room where all the widows stood by him weeping, displaying the coats and clothing which Dorcas had made while she was with them. But

Peter sent them out of the room and kneeled down and prayed, and turning to the body, he said, "Tabitha, arise." And she opened her eyes and when she saw Peter, she sat up. Then he gave her his hand and helped her up and calling the saints and widows, he presented her alive. And it became known throughout all Joppa and many believed in the Lord. And it came to pass that he stayed in Joppa for many days with a tanner named Simon.

Now there was a certain man in Caesarea named Cornelius, a centurion of what was called the Italian Regiment. He was a devout man, one that feared God with his whole household and gave much charity to the people, praying to God continually. He saw clearly in a vision, at about the ninth hour of the day, an angel of God coming to him and saying, "Cornelius." But when he saw him, he was afraid and said, "What is it, Lord?" He said to him, "Your prayers and your charity have come up into remembrance before God. Now therefore send men to Joppa and ask for Simon, who is also called Peter. He is staying with Simon, a tanner whose house is by the seaside. He will tell you what you ought to do." And when the angel which was speaking to Cornelius had departed, he called two of his servants and a soldier that feared God out of those that waited on him. When he had told them everything, he sent them to Joppa.

The next day, as they were going on their journey and drawing near to the city, Peter went up on the house to pray at about the sixth hour. Then he became hungry and wanted to eat, and while they were preparing the food, he fell into a trance. He saw heaven opened and some object coming down to him—something like a great sheet fastened at the four corners being let down to the earth. Inside it were all kinds of four footed animals of the earth, wild beasts, crawling things, and birds of the air. And there came a voice to him: "Get up, Peter. Kill and eat." But Peter said, "Not so, Lord, because I have never eaten anything that is common or unclean." And the voice spoke to him again a second time: "Do not consider unclean the things that God has made clean." This happened three times and the object was taken up again into heaven.

While Peter wondered to himself what this vision which he had seen meant, behold, the men which were sent from Cornelius, had found Simon's house and stood at the gate. They called and asked whether Simon, which was also called Peter, was staying there. While Peter thought about the vision, the Spirit said to him, "Behold, three men are looking for you. Therefore, get up, go downstairs and go with them and do not doubt, because I have sent them." Then Peter went down to the men who had been sent to him from Cornelius and said, "Behold, I am the one whom you seek. What is the reason for which you have come?" And they said, "Cornelius the centurion—a righteous and God-fearing man, who has a good report among the entire nation of the Jews—was warned from heaven by a holy angel to send for you to come to his house and to hear your words." Then he invited them in and gave them lodging. The next day, Peter went with them and some of the brethren from Joppa accompanied him.

The following day, they entered into Caesarea. Cornelius was waiting for them and had called together his family and close friends. And it happened that as Peter came in, Cornelius met him and fell down at his feet and worshiped him. But Peter lifted him up, saying, "Stand up, I myself am also a man." And as he talked with him, he entered and found many that had come together. And he said to them, "You know that it is an unlawful thing for a man who is a Jew to keep company or to visit with one of another nation, but God has showed me that I should not call any man common or unclean. Therefore, I came to you without refusing when I was sent for. I ask though, for what reason have you sent for me?"

Then Cornelius said, "Four days ago, at about this hour, I fasted and at the ninth hour I prayed in my house, and behold, a man stood in front of me in bright clothing. He said, 'Cornelius, your prayer is heard and your charity is held in remembrance in the sight of God. Therefore, send to Joppa and ask for Simon, who is also called Peter. He is staying in the house of Simon, a tanner by the seaside. When he comes, he will speak to you.' Then I sent for you immediately and you have done well to come. Now then, we are all here before God to hear all the things commanded you by God."

Then Peter opened his mouth and said, "In truth, I perceive that God is no respecter of persons, but in every nation the one that fears him and works righteousness is accepted with him. You know the word which God has sent to the children of Israel—preaching peace through Jesus Christ, who is Lord of all—the word which came through all Judea, beginning in Galilee after the baptism which John preached: how God anointed Jesus of Nazareth with the holy Ghost and with power, and how he went about doing good and healing all that were oppressed of the devil because God was with him. We are witnesses of all the things which he did, both in the land of the Jews and in Jerusalem, and how they killed him, hanging him on a tree. God raised him up the third day and showed him openly, not to all the people, but to the witnesses God had chosen beforehand, that is, to those of us which ate and drank with him after he arose from the dead. He commanded us to preach to the people and to testify that he was ordained by God to be a judge of the living and the dead. The prophets also give witness to him, that through his Name all that believe in him shall receive remission of sins."

While Peter was speaking these words, the holy Ghost fell on all of them which heard the word. Those of the circumcision which believed were astonished, as many as came with Peter, because the gift of the holy Ghost was being poured out on the Gentiles. They heard them speaking with tongues and magnifying God. Then Peter said, "Can any man withhold water, that these which have received the holy Ghost should not be baptized, as well as we?" So he commanded them to be baptized in the Name of the Lord. Then they asked him to stay a few days.

Now the apostles and the brethren that were in Judea, heard that the Gentiles had also received the word of God. And when Peter had come up to Jerusalem, those of the circumcision argued with him, saying, "You went to uncircumcised men, and have eaten with them." Then Peter began to explain the thing in order to them, saying, "I was in the city of Joppa, praying, and in a trance I saw a vision of an object coming down like a great sheet being let down from heaven by the four corners. It came towards me and when I had fixed my eyes on it, I saw four footed animals of the earth, wild beasts, crawling things, and birds of the air. I also heard a voice saying to me, 'Get up, Peter. Kill and eat.' And I said, 'God forbid, Lord, because nothing common or unclean has entered into my mouth at anytime.' But the voice answered me a second time from heaven, 'Do not call unclean the things that God has made clean.' And this happened three times and everything was taken up again into heaven. Then behold, immediately there were three men that had come to the house where I was, sent to me from Caesarea. And the Spirit said to me that I should go with them without doubting. Moreover, these six brothers came with me and we entered into the man's house. He told us how he had seen an angel in his house, which stood and said to him, 'Send men to Joppa and call for Simon, who is also called Peter. He will speak words to you by which both you and your entire household will be saved.' And as I began to speak, the holy Ghost fell upon them, just as upon us at the beginning. Then I remembered the word of the Lord and how he said, 'John baptized with water, but you shall be baptized with the holy Ghost.' For as much then as God gave the same gift to them as he gave to us when we believed in the Lord Jesus Christ, who was I that I could withstand God?" When they heard these things, they held their peace and glorified God, saying, "Then God has also granted repentance unto life to the Gentiles."

Then those which were scattered abroad because of the persecution that arose because of Stephen, traveled as far as Phoenicia and Cyprus and Antioch, preaching the word to no one except to the Jews only. But some of them were men of Cyprus and of Cyrene, which when they had come into Antioch, spoke to the Hellenists and preached the Lord Jesus. And the hand of the Lord was with them, so that a great number believed and turned to the Lord. Then news of those things was heard by the church in Jerusalem, and they sent Barnabas, that he should go to Antioch. When he arrived and had seen the grace of God, he was glad and encouraged all of them that with a resolute heart they should continue in the Lord. He was a good man and full of the holy Ghost and faith, and many people were being added to the Lord.

Then Barnabas departed to Tarsus to look for Saul, and when he had found him he brought him to Antioch. And so it happened that for a whole year they were gathered with the church and taught many people, so much so that the disciples were first called Christians in Antioch. In those days, prophets also came from Jerusalem to Antioch. One of them named Agabus stood up and signified by the Spirit that there would be a great famine throughout all the world, which also came to pass under Claudius Caesar. Then the disciples, each one according to his ability, determined to send relief to the brethren which lived in Judea. This very thing they did, sending it to the elders by the hands of Barnabas and Saul.

Herod Imprisons Peter

Now about that time, Herod the king stretched forth his hand to punish some of the church. He killed James the brother of John with the sword. When he saw that it pleased the Jews, he continued and also arrested Peter during the days of unleavened bread. When he had caught him, he put him in prison, and handed him over to four squads of soldiers to be guarded, intending to bring him out to the people after the Passover. So Peter was kept in prison, but prayers were earnestly being made unto God for him by the church. And when Herod wanted to have him brought out to the people, the same night Peter slept between two soldiers, bound with two chains, while the guards at the door watched over the prison. And behold, the angel of the Lord came upon them and a light shined in the cell, and he struck Peter on the side and woke him up, saying, "Get up quickly." His chains fell off of his hands and the angel said to him, "Dress yourself and put on your sandals." And so he did. Then he said to him, "Wrap your coat around you and follow me." So Peter came out and followed him, not understanding that what the angel had done for him was real, thinking he had seen a vision. Now when they were past the first and the second guard, they came to the iron gate that leads out into the city and it opened to them of its own accord, and they went out and passed through one street, and immediately the angel departed from him. When Peter came to himself, he said, "Now I know for sure that the Lord has sent his angel and has delivered me out of Herod's hand and from all that the Jewish people were expecting."

As he considered this, he came to the house of Mary the mother of John, who is also called Mark, where many were gathered together and praying. When Peter knocked at the entry door, a maid named Rhoda answered, but when she recognized Peter's voice, she did not open the entry door, but ran in with joy, announcing that Peter was standing at the door. But they said to her, "You are out of your mind." Yet she kept insisting that it was true. Then they said, "It is his angel." But Peter continued knocking and when they had opened it, they saw him and were astonished. And he motioned to them with his hand to keep their peace, and told them how the Lord had brought him out of the prison. And he said, "Go tell these things to James and to the brethren." Then he departed and went to another place.

Now as soon as it was morning, there was no small disturbance among the soldiers about what had become of Peter. When Herod searched for him and could not find him, he questioned the guards and commanded that they should be put to death. And he went down from Judea to Caesarea and stayed there.

Then Herod became angry with the people of Tyre and Sidon, but they all came to him with one accord and persuaded Blastus, the king's chamberlain, that they desired peace, because their country was fed by the king's land. And on an appointed day, Herod arrayed himself in royal apparel and sat on the throne and gave a speech to them. And the people began to shout, saying, "The voice of a god, and not of a man." And immediately the angel of the Lord struck him, because he did not give glory to God, and he was eaten by worms and breathed his last. And the word of God grew and multiplied.

Barnabas and Paul

Barnabas and Saul returned from Jerusalem when they had completed their service, and took with them John, who is also called Mark. There were also other prophets and teachers in the church at Antioch: Barnabas, Simeon called Niger, Lucius of Cyrene, Manaen (who had been brought up with Herod the tetrarch), and Saul. As they were ministering to the Lord and fasting, the holy Ghost said, "Separate unto me Barnabas and Saul for the work to which I have called them." Then they fasted and prayed and laid their hands on them and sent them out. After they had been sent forth by the holy Ghost, they came down to Seleucia and from there they sailed to Cyprus. And when they were at Salamis, they preached the word of God in the synagogues of the Jews, and John was also assisting them.

When they had gone throughout the island as far as Paphos, they found a certain sorcerer, a Jewish false prophet named Bar-Jesus, who was with the proconsul Sergius Paulus, a man of intelligence. He called Barnabas and Saul to him and desired to hear the word of God. But Elymas the sorcerer (for so is his name translated) withstood them, and tried to turn the proconsul away from the faith. Then Saul, who is also called Paul, being full of the holy Ghost, fixed his eyes on him and said, "O full of all deceit and all fraud, you child of the devil and enemy of all righteousness, will you not cease perverting the straight ways of the Lord? Now therefore behold, the hand of the Lord is upon you, and you shall be blind and not see the sun for a time." Immediately a mist and a darkness fell upon him and he went about seeking someone to lead him by the hand. When the proconsul saw what had happened, he believed and was astonished by the doctrine of the Lord.

Now after Paul and those with him had departed from Paphos by ship, they came to Perga, a city of Pamphylia; and John departed from them and returned to Jerusalem. When they departed from Perga they came to Antioch, a city of Pisidia and went into the synagogue and sat down on the Sabbath day. After the reading of the Law and Prophets, the rulers of the synagogue sent word to them, saying, "Men and brothers, if you have any word of exhortation for the people, say it." Then Paul stood up and motioned with his hand and said, "Men of Israel and you who fear God, listen. The God of the people of Israel chose our fathers and exalted the people when they lived in the land of Egypt, and brought them out of there with his strong arm. And for about forty years, he put up with their behavior in the wilderness. He destroyed seven nations in the land of Canaan and divided the land among them by allotment. After this he gave judges to them for about four hundred and fifty years, until the time of Samuel the prophet. After this they desired a king and God gave them Saul—the son of Cis, a man of the tribe of Benjamin—for forty years. After he had taken him away, he raised up David to be their king, of whom he witnessed and said, 'I have found David the son of Jesse, a man after my own heart, who will do all my will.' From this man's descendants, according to his promise, God raised up for Israel the Savior, Jesus, after John had first preached the baptism of repentance to all the people of Israel before his coming. As John was completing his ministry, he said, 'Whom do you think that I am? I am not him, but behold, there will come one after me whose shoes I am not worthy to untie.' Men and brothers, children of the generation of Abraham, and as many among you that fear God, the word of this salvation is sent to you."

"Those who live in Jerusalem and their rulers, because they neither knew him nor the words of the prophets which are read every Sabbath day, have fulfilled them by condemning him. And though they found no reason worthy of death in him, yet they asked Pilate to have him put to death. And when they had fulfilled all the things that were written about him, they took him down from the tree and placed him in a tomb. But God raised him up from the dead and he was seen for many days by those who came up with him from Galilee to Jerusalem, and they are now his witnesses to the people. We declare to you that regarding the promise made to the fathers, God has fulfilled it among us, their children, in that he raised up Jesus, just as it is written in the second Psalm, 'You are my Son; today I have begotten you.' And as for the fact that he raised him up from the dead, no more to return to corruption, he has said this, 'I will give you the holy things of David, which are faithful.' Also in another place he said, 'You will not allow your holy one to see corruption.' Indeed, David, after serving his time by the will of God, slept and was laid with his fathers and saw corruption. But the One whom God raised up saw no corruption. Therefore, men and brothers, let it be known to you that through this man is the forgiveness of sins preached unto you. And from all things from which you could not be justified by the Law of Moses, by him everyone that believes is justified. Be on your guard, therefore, lest the thing which is spoken of by the prophets will come upon you: 'Behold, you skeptics, be astonished and perish, because I will do a work in your days, a work which you will not believe, even if a man declares it unto you.'"

When they had come out of the synagogue of the Jews, the Gentiles begged that they would preach these words to them on the next Sabbath day. And when the crowd had dissolved, many of the Jews and converts that feared God followed Paul and Barnabas, who spoke to them and encouraged them to continue in the grace of God. And on the next Sabbath day nearly the whole city was gathered together to hear the word of God. When the Jews saw the people, they were filled with envy and began speaking against what Paul was saying by contradicting and insulting him. Then Paul and Barnabas spoke boldly and said, "It was necessary for the word of God to have been spoken to you first, but since you push it away and judge yourselves unworthy of everlasting life, we will now turn to the Gentiles. For the Lord has commanded us, saying, 'I have made you a light for the Gentiles, that you should bring salvation to the ends of the world.'" Now when the Gentiles heard this, they were glad and glorified the word of the Lord; and as many as were ordained to eternal life, believed. Thus the word of the Lord was being spread throughout the whole country.

The Jews began stirring up some of the devout and honorable women and the leading men of the city, raising up persecution against Paul and Barnabas and forcing them out of their regions. But they shook off the dust of their feet against them and came to Iconium; and the disciples were filled with joy and with the holy Ghost. It happened in Iconium that both of them went together into the synagogue of the Jews and spoke, such that a large number of both the Jews and the Hellenists believed. But the unbelieving Jews stirred up and poisoned the minds of the Gentiles against the brethren. Therefore they stayed there a long time, speaking boldly in the Lord and giving testimony to the word of his grace, granting signs and wonders to be done by their hands. But the people of the city were divided; some were with the Jews and some with the apostles. And when there was a violent attempt to hurt and to stone them made by the Gentiles and the Jews and their rulers, they were made aware of it and fled to Lystra and Derbe—cities of Lycaonia and the region around it—and preached the Gospel there.

Now a certain man sat in Lystra who was lame in his feet; he was crippled from his mother's womb and had never walked. He heard Paul speak and when Paul saw him and realized that he had faith to be healed, he said with a loud voice, "Stand up on your feet." And he jumped up and walked. When the people saw what Paul had done, they lifted up their voices, saying in the language of Lycaonia, "Gods have come down to us in the likeness of men." And Barnabas they called Zeus and Paul they called Hermes, because he was the chief speaker. Then Zeus's priest, who was outside the city, brought bulls with garlands to the gates, wanting to sacrifice along with the people. But when Barnabas and Paul heard about it, they tore their clothes and ran in among the people, crying and saying, "Men, why are you doing these things? We are also men with the same nature as you, and we are preaching unto you that you should turn from these worthless things to the living God, who made heaven and earth and the sea and all things that are in them. In times past, he has allowed the Gentiles to walk in their own ways, but he did not leave himself without a witness, in that he did good for us by giving rain from heaven and fruitful seasons, and filled our hearts with food and gladness." Even after speaking these things, they could hardly convince the crowd to not sacrifice to them.

Then some Jews came from Antioch and Iconium who persuaded the people to stone Paul. Then they threw him out of the city, thinking he was dead. However, as the disciples stood around him, he stood up and came into the city, and the next day he departed with Barnabas to Derbe. After they had preached the good news of the Gospel to that city and taught many, they returned to Lystra and to Iconium and to Antioch, strengthening the disciples' hearts and encouraging them to continue in the faith, affirming that through many afflictions must they enter into the kingdom of God. And when they had ordained elders for them by election in every church and prayed and fasted, they commended them to the Lord in whom they believed. Thus they went throughout Pisidia and came to Pamphylia, and after they had preached the word in Perga, they came down to Attalia, and from there sailed to Antioch, from where they had been commended to the grace of God and to the work which they had fulfilled. And when they had come and gathered the church together, they told of all the things that God had done through them and how he had opened the door of faith to the Gentiles. So they stayed there a long time with the disciples.

The Council at Jerusalem

Then some men came down from Judea and taught the brethren, saying, "Unless you are circumcised in the manner of Moses, you cannot be saved." When there was much disagreement and dispute by Paul and Barnabas against them, they determined that Paul and Barnabas and some of the others should go up to the apostles and elders in Jerusalem about this question. Being sent out by the church, they passed through Phoenicia and Samaria and declared to them the conversion of the Gentiles and brought great joy to all the brethren. When they arrived in Jerusalem, they were received by the church and by the apostles and elders, and they told of the things God had done through them. But they said that some of the sect of the Pharisees who had believed stood up and said that it was necessary for them to be circumcised and commanded to keep the Law of Moses.

Then the apostles and elders gathered together to look into this matter. And when there had been great disagreement, Peter rose up and said to them, "Men and brothers, you know that a good while ago God chose me out from among us, that from my mouth the Gentiles should hear the word of the Gospel and believe. And God, who knows the heart, bore witness to this by giving the holy Ghost to them, even as he did to us. And he made no difference between us and them after he had purified their hearts by faith. Now therefore, why do you tempt God by laying a yoke on the disciples' necks which neither our fathers nor we were able to bear? We believe that it is through the grace of the Lord Jesus Christ that we are saved, and so do they."

Then all of them kept quiet and listened to Barnabas and Paul, who told what signs and wonders God had done among the Gentiles through them. When they held their peace, James answered and said, "Men and brothers, listen to me. Simon has told us how God first visited the Gentiles to take from them a people for his own Name. And with this the words of the prophets agree, as it is written, 'After this I will return and build again the tabernacle of David, which has fallen down; and the ruins of it I will build again, and I will set it up, so that the rest of mankind might seek after the Lord, and all the Gentiles who are called by my Name, says the Lord who does all these things.' From the beginning of the world, God knew all his works. Therefore my judgment is that we trouble the Gentiles that have turned to God no further, but that we send word to them that they keep themselves from the pollution of idols, from fornication, from what has been strangled, and from blood. For Moses has been preached for many generations in every city, seeing as he is read in the synagogues every Sabbath day.

Then it seemed good to the apostles and elders with the whole church to send men chosen from among them to Antioch with Paul and Barnabas—Judas who was also called Barsabas, and Silas—who were leading men among the brethren. They wrote this letter for them:

> To the brothers which are Gentiles in Antioch, Syria, and Cilicia, the apostles and the elders and the brethren send you greetings. We have been told that some have gone out from among us and have troubled you with words and burdened your minds by saying that you must be circumcised and keep the Law, yet we gave no such commandment. Therefore, it seemed good to us, after we had come together with one accord, to send chosen men with our beloved Barnabas and Paul to you; men that have given up their lives for the Name of our Lord Jesus Christ. We have therefore sent Judas and Silas, who shall also tell you the same things in person.
>
> It seemed good to the holy Ghost, and to us, to lay no more burden upon you than these necessary things. That is, that you keep yourself from things offered to idols, and blood, and that which is strangled, and from fornication. If you keep yourselves from such things, you shall do well. *Farewell.*

Now after they had departed and arrived in Antioch, they gathered the congregation together and delivered the letter to them. When they had read it, they rejoiced because of its encouragement, and since Judas and Silas were prophets, they encouraged and strengthened the brethren with many words. And after they had stayed there a while, the brethren sent them back to the apostles in peace; however, it seemed good to Silas to stay there. Also, Paul and

Barnabas remained in Antioch, teaching and preaching the word of the Lord with many others.

Then after some days Paul said to Barnabas, "Let us return and visit our brothers in every city where we have preached the word of the Lord and see how they are doing." Barnabas wanted to take John with them, called Mark. But Paul insisted that it was not good to take him with them because he had departed from them at Pamphylia and did not go with them to the work. Their disagreement became sharp such that they departed from one another, and Barnabas took Mark and sailed to Cyprus. Paul chose Silas and departed, being committed by the brethren to the grace of God; and he went through Syria and Cilicia, strengthening the churches.

Paul and Silas

Then he came to Derbe and to Lystra, and behold, a certain disciple named Timothy was there. He was the son of a Jewish woman who believed, but his father was Greek. He was well spoken of by the brethren in Lystra and Iconium. Therefore, Paul wanted him to go with him, and took and circumcised him because of the Jews which were in those parts and they all knew that his father was Greek. And as they went through the cities, they delivered to them the decrees to keep which had been determined by the apostles and elders which were in Jerusalem. And so the churches were strengthened in the faith and were daily being increased in number.

Now when they had gone throughout Phrygia and the region of Galatia, they were forbidden by the holy Ghost to preach the word in Asia. Then they came to Mysia and tried to go into Bithynia, but the Spirit did not allow them. Therefore they passed through Mysia and came down to Troas, where Paul had a vision appear to him in the night. A man from Macedonia stood there and pleaded with him, saying, "Come to Macedonia and help us." After he had seen the vision, we immediately prepared to go to Macedonia, being confident that the Lord had called us to preach the Gospel to them. Then we left Troas and with a straight course came to Samothrace, and the next day came to Neapolis. And from there to Philippi, which is the foremost city in that part of Macedonia, where citizens from Rome had come to live. We stayed in that city for several days, and on the Sabbath day we went outside the city, next to a river, where they were accustomed to pray. We sat down and spoke to the women which had come together. Then a certain woman named Lydia, a seller of purple from the city of Thyatira, came and was worshiping God. When she heard us, the Lord opened her heart to listen to the things which Paul was saying. And after she was baptized with her household, she begged us, saying, "If you have judged me to be faithful to the Lord, come to my house and stay there." And she prevailed upon us.

Then it happened that as we went to prayer, a certain slave girl met us, she had a spirit of divination and brought her masters much profit by telling fortunes. She followed Paul and us and cried, saying, "These men are servants of the most high God, proclaiming to you the way of salvation." And she did this for many days, but Paul, being greatly annoyed, turned around and said to the spirit, "I command you in the Name of Jesus Christ, that you come out of her." And he came out that very hour. Now when her masters saw that the hope of their profit was gone, they caught Paul and Silas and dragged them to the marketplace before the magistrates. They brought them to the governors, saying, "These men which are Jews trouble our city and preach customs which are neither lawful for us to receive nor to observe, since we are Romans." The people also rose up together against them and the governors tore their clothes and commanded them to be beaten with rods. And when they had beaten them repeatedly, they threw them into prison, commanding the jailer to keep them securely. Having received this commandment, he threw them into the inner prison and fastened their feet in the stocks.

At midnight, Paul and Silas were praying and singing psalms to God and the prisoners were listening to them. Suddenly there was a great earthquake and the foundation of the prison was shaken, and all the doors immediately opened and every man's chains were loosed. Then the keeper of the prison awoke from his sleep, and when he saw the prison doors open, he drew out his sword to kill himself, assuming the prisoners had all fled. But Paul cried with a loud voice, saying, "Do not harm yourself, we are all here." Then he called for a light and rushed in, and came trembling and fell down before Paul and Silas. And he brought them out and said, "Sirs, what must I do to be saved?" And they said, "Believe in the Lord Jesus Christ and you will be saved, you and your household." And they preached the word of the Lord to him and to all that were in his house. Afterward, he took them the same hour of the night and washed their stripes and was baptized right away with all that belonged to him. When he had brought them to his house, he set food in front of them and rejoiced that he and his whole household believed in God.

When it was morning, the governors sent the officers, saying, "Let those men go." Then the keeper of the prison told this to Paul, saying, "The governors have sent to let you go. Now, therefore, depart and go in peace." Then Paul said to them, "After they have publicly beaten us—as uncondemned Romans—and have cast us into prison, now they want to put us out secretly? No indeed, let them come and bring us out." And the officers told these words to the governors, who became afraid when they heard that they were Romans. Then they came and pleaded with them and brought them out, asking them to depart out of the city. And they left the prison and entered into the house of Lydia, and after they had seen the brethren, they encouraged them and departed.

Now as they passed through Amphipolis and Apollonia, they

came to Thessalonica, where a synagogue of the Jews was located. And as his custom was, Paul went in and reasoned with them for three Sabbath days regarding the Scriptures, explaining and proving that Christ must have suffered and risen again from the dead, and that this is Jesus Christ, whom, he said, "I am preaching to you." Some of them believed and joined with Paul and Silas, also a great many of the God-fearing Greeks, and a number of the leading women. But the unbelieving Jews became envious and gathered ruffians and wicked men and brought them together in a mob and created uproar in the city; and they attacked the house of Jason, seeking to bring them out to the people. But when they did not find them, they dragged Jason and some of the brethren before the rulers of the city, shouting, "The ones who have turned the world upside down are now here, and Jason has welcomed them. They are defying the decrees of Caesar by saying that there is another King, who is Jesus." Then the people and the rulers of the city were disturbed when they heard these things. Nevertheless, when they had received enough assurance from Jason and the others, they let them go. And immediately that night the brethren sent Paul and Silas away to Berea. When they arrived there, they entered into the synagogue of the Jews. These men were more noble than those in Thessalonica and received the word with eagerness, searching the Scriptures daily to see whether these things were so. Therefore many of them believed, some of which were prominent women and men of the Greeks.

When the Jews in Thessalonica found out that the word of God was being preached by Paul in Berea, they also came there and stirred up the people. But the brethren quickly sent Paul away, to go to the sea, but Silas and Timothy remained there. And those which were escorting Paul brought him to Athens, and after receiving the message that Silas and Timothy should join him as soon as possible, they departed. While Paul waited for them in Athens, his spirit was provoked within him when he saw that the city was filled with idols. Therefore he reasoned in the synagogue with the Jews and with those worshiping, and also with everyone he met each day in the market. When certain philosophers of the Epicureans and the Stoics disputed with him, some said, "What will this babbler say?" Others said, "He seems to be a proclaimer of strange gods"—because he was preaching Jesus and the resurrection to them. Then they took him and brought him to the Hill of Ares, saying, "May we know what this new doctrine is of which you are speaking? You are bringing some strange things to our ears, and therefore we want to know what they mean." All the Athenians and the visitors which stayed there gave themselves to nothing else but to the telling or hearing of something new.

Then Paul stood in the middle of the Hill of Ares and said, "Men of Athens, I perceive that in all things you are very religious, because as I walked around and looked at your objects of worship, I found an altar on which was written, 'TO THE UNKNOWN GOD.' Him whom you worship in ignorance, I will show unto you. The God that made the world and all things that are in it—since he is Lord of heaven and earth—does not dwell in temples made by hands. Neither is he worshiped by men's hands as though he needed anything. He gives life and breath to everything and has made all mankind from one blood to live on all the face of the earth. He has determined the times which were ordained for them and the boundaries of their habitation that they would seek the Lord and would indeed reach out and find him, although he is not far from any of us. For in him we live and move and have our being, as some of your own poets have also said: 'For we are also his children.' Seeing as how we are the children of God, we should not think that the Godhead is like gold or silver or stone, crafted by art or the invention of man. God has therefore overlooked these former times of ignorance, but now he commands all men everywhere to repent, because he has fixed a day in which he will judge the world in righteousness, by the man whom he has appointed. And he has given assurance of this to all men in that he has raised him from the dead."

Now some mocked when they heard of the resurrection from the dead, but others said, "We will hear you again of this thing." And so Paul departed from among them. However, some of them joined him and believed; among them Dionysius from the Hill of Ares, a woman named Damaris, and others with them.

After these things, Paul departed from Athens and came to Corinth. There he met a certain Jew named Aquila, a native of Pontus who had recently come from Italy with his wife Priscilla, because Claudius had commanded all Jews to leave Rome. Since they had the same trade, he stayed with them and worked (they were tent-makers). And every Sabbath day he reasoned in the synagogue and encouraged the Jews and the Greeks. When Silas and Timothy arrived from Macedonia, Paul was compelled by the Spirit and testified to the Jews that Jesus was the Christ. And when they resisted and blasphemed, he shook his garments and said to them, "Your blood is on your own heads; I am clean. From now on, I will go to the Gentiles." So he left there and entered into a certain man's house who was named Justus; he was a worshiper of God and his house was next to the synagogue. Crispus, the chief ruler of the synagogue, believed in the Lord with his whole household, and when many of the Corinthians heard about it, they believed and were baptized. Then the Lord said to Paul through a vision in the night, "Do not fear, but speak. Do not hold your peace because I am with you. No man shall lay his hands on you to hurt you because I have many people in this city." So he stayed there a year and six months, teaching the word of God among them.

When Gallio was proconsul of Achaia, the Jews rose up with one accord against Paul and brought him to the judgment seat, saying, "This fellow is convincing men to worship God in ways contrary to the Law." As Paul was about to open his mouth, Gallio said to the Jews, "If it were a matter of wrongdoing or evil deeds, O Jews, I would have a reason to hear your complaint. But if it is a question of words and names and of your Law, look into it for yourselves, for I will not be a judge of those things." And he drove them away from the judgment seat. Then all the Greeks took Sosthenes, the chief ruler of the synagogue, and beat him in front of the judgment seat, but Gallio cared nothing about those things.

After Paul had stayed there for a long while, he departed from the brethren and sailed into Syria, and Priscilla and Aquila went with him. After this, he shaved his head in Cenchrea because he had made a vow. Then he came to Ephesus and left them there, but he entered into the synagogue and reasoned with the Jews. They wanted him to stay with them for a longer time, but he would not consent and bade them farewell, saying, "I must keep the feast that is coming in Jerusalem, but I will return to you again if God wills it. So he sailed from Ephesus.

When he came down to Caesarea, he went up to Jerusalem, and after he had greeted the church, he went down to Antioch. After he had stayed there a while, he departed and went from place to place in the region of Galatia and Phrygia, strengthening all the disciples. And a certain Jew named Apollos, a native of Alexandria, came to Ephesus. He was an eloquent man and mighty in the Scriptures. He was instructed in the way of the Lord and he spoke fervently in the Spirit, diligently teaching the things of the Lord, but knew only of the baptism of John. And he began to speak boldly in the synagogue, and when Aquila and Priscilla heard him, they took him aside and explained to him the way of God more perfectly. And when he wanted to go to Achaia, the brethren encouraged him and wrote to the disciples to receive him. After he arrived there, he helped many of them which had believed through grace, because he powerfully refuted the Jews in public, showing by the Scriptures that Jesus was the Christ.

While Apollos was in Corinth, it happened that when Paul passed through the upper coasts and came to Ephesus, he found some disciples and said to them, "Have you received the holy Ghost since you believed?" And they said to him, "We have not even heard whether there is a holy Ghost." And he said to them, "What were you baptized into then?" And they said, "Into John's baptism." Then Paul said, "John indeed baptized with the baptism of repentance, saying to the people that they should believe in the One to come after him, that is, in Christ Jesus." And when they heard this, they were baptized into the Name of the Lord Jesus. And Paul laid hands on them and the holy Ghost came upon them, and they spoke with tongues and prophesied. And there were about twelve men in all.

Then he went into the synagogue and spoke boldly for three months, reasoning and persuading regarding the things that apply to the kingdom of God. But when some became hardened and disobeyed and spoke evil of the way of God before the crowd, he departed from them and took the disciples with him, and reasoned each day in the school of one Tyrannus. This continued for two years, so that all of them which dwelt in Asia heard the word of the Lord Jesus, both Jews and Greeks.

And God was performing powerful miracles by the hands of Paul, so that aprons and handkerchiefs were brought from his body to the sick, and the diseases departed and the evil spirits went out of them. Then some of the Jewish exorcists, who would travel from place to place, undertook to name the Name of the Lord Jesus over those which had evil spirits, saying, "We adjure you by Jesus, whom Paul preaches." And there were seven sons of Sceva, a Jewish priest, which were doing this. And the evil spirit answered and said, "Jesus I know and Paul I know, but who are you?" And the man in whom the evil spirit was jumped on them, overpowering and prevailing against them, so that they ran out of the house naked and wounded. And this became known to all the Jews and Greeks which dwelt in Ephesus, and fear came over all of them and the Name of the Lord Jesus was magnified. And many believed and came, confessing and declaring their deeds. Also, many of them which practiced magic brought their books and burned them in front of everyone; and they counted up the price of them and found it to be fifty thousand pieces of silver. So the word of God grew mightily and prevailed.

After this, Paul purposed by the Spirit to pass through Macedonia and Achaia and to go to Jerusalem, saying, "After I have been there, I must also see Rome." So he sent two of them that were with him, Timothy and Erastus, to Macedonia, but he remained in Asia for a while. And at this time there arose a great commotion about the Way, because of a certain silversmith named Demetrius, who made silver shrines of Diana and brought great profits to the craftsmen. He called them together along with the workmen of similar things and said, "Sirs, you know that we have made our wealth because of this business. Moreover, you see and hear that not only in Ephesus, but throughout almost all of Asia, this Paul has convinced and turned many people away by saying that gods made with the hands are not gods at all. It is not only that our trade is in danger of being discredited, but also that the temple of the great goddess Diana would no longer be esteemed, and that it would happen that her magnificence, which all Asia and the world worships, would be destroyed."

Now when they heard this, they were full of rage and cried out, saying, "Great is Diana of the Ephesians." And the whole city became filled with confusion, and they rushed into the theater with one accord and caught Gaius and Aristarchus, who were from Macedonia and were companions of Paul on his journey. When Paul wanted to go in to the people, the disciples would not allow him. Some of the leaders of Asia who were his friends, sent to him also, pleading with him to not present himself in the theater. Some therefore cried one thing and others another thing because the crowd was out of control, and most of them did not even know why they were there. Someone in the crowd drew Alexander out and the Jews began pushing him forward. Alexander then motioned with his hand, wishing to explain the matter to the people. But when they recognized that he was a Jew, a shout went up for nearly two hours, with everyone crying, "Great is Diana of the Ephesians." Then after he had quieted the people, the city clerk said, "Men of Ephesus, what man does not know that the city of the Ephesians guards the temple of the great goddess Diana and of the image which came down from Zeus? Seeing then that no one can speak against these things, you should calm yourselves and not act foolishly. You have brought these men here, but they have committed neither sacrilege, nor have they blasphemed your goddess. Therefore, if Demetrius and the craftsmen have a complaint against anyone, the courts are open and the proconsuls are there, let them accuse one another. But if you have inquiries concerning other matters, it will be settled by a lawful assembly. We are even in danger of being accused of sedition today, seeing as how there is no reason that we could give to justify all this commotion." And after he had spoken this, he dismissed the people.

Now after the uproar had ceased, Paul called the disciples to him, embraced them and departed for Macedonia. When he had gone through that region and had encouraged them with many words, he arrived in Greece and stayed there for three months. The Jews were lying in wait for him as he was about to sail into Syria, so he decided to return through Macedonia. There he was accompanied into Asia by Sopater from Berea, and by Aristarchus and Secundus from Thessalonica, and Gaius from Derbe, and Timothy, and Tychicus and Trophimus from Asia. These men went ahead and waited for us at Troas. We sailed out of Philippi after the days of unleavened bread, and joined them in Troas five days later and stayed there for seven days.

On the first day of the week, when the disciples came together to break bread, Paul was preaching to them. He was ready to depart the next day and he continued preaching until midnight. There were many lights in the upper room where they were gathered together. And a certain young man, named Eutychus, was sitting there in a window and falling into a deep sleep, and as Paul kept preaching he was overcome by sleep and fell down from the third story, and was picked up dead. But Paul went down and fell upon him and embraced him, saying, "Do not be troubled, for his life is yet in him." Then when Paul came up again and had broken bread and eaten, he continued speaking until morning, and then he departed. And they brought the boy in alive, and they were greatly comforted.

Then we went ahead to the ship and sailed to the city of Assos, so that we might meet Paul there, because he had decided that he would go on foot. Now when he met us in Assos, we brought him on board and came to Mitylene. Sailing from there, we came the next day opposite Chios, and the next day arrived at Samos, and stayed in Trogyllium. The following day we came to Miletus. Paul had decided to sail past Ephesus, because he did not want to spend time in Asia. He was anxious, if it was possible, to be in Jerusalem for the day of Pentecost. Therefore from Miletus, he sent to Ephesus and called the elders of the church. When they arrived, he said to them, "You know from the first day that I came to Asia, in what way I have always lived among you, serving the Lord with all humility, and with many tears and trials which came upon me by the scheming of the Jews, and how I held back nothing that was profitable for you, and have showed you and taught you publicly and in every house, declaring both to the Jews and to the Greeks the repentance toward God and faith toward our Lord Jesus Christ. And behold, now I am bound by the Spirit to go to Jerusalem, and do not know what things shall happen to me there, except that the holy Ghost is testifying in every city and saying that chains and tribulations await me. But I am not moved, neither do I count my life as dear to myself, so that I may finish my race with joy and the work which I have received of the Lord Jesus: to testify to the Gospel of the grace of God."

"Now behold, I know that from now on, all of you through whom I have gone preaching the kingdom of God shall not see my face again. Therefore I am assuring you today that I am innocent of the blood of all men, because I have held nothing back, and have proclaimed to you the whole counsel of God. Therefore, take heed to yourselves, and to all of the flock over which the holy Ghost has made you overseers, to feed the church of God which he has purchased with his own blood. For I know that after my departure, savage wolves will enter in among you, not sparing the flock. Further, from among you men will arise, speaking perverse things, to draw disciples away after them. Therefore watch and remember that for three years I did not cease to warn everyone both night and day with tears. And now brothers, I commit you to God and to the word of his grace, which is able to build you up and give you an inheritance among all of them which are sanctified. I have coveted no one's silver, nor gold, nor clothing. Yes, you well know that these hands have ministered to my own needs and to those with me. I have showed you in every way that by laboring we support the weak. Remember the words of the Lord Jesus, how he said that it is more blessed to give than it is to receive."

When he said this, he kneeled down and prayed with all of them. Then they all wept greatly, and fell on Paul's neck and kissed him. They were especially grieved because he said that they would not see his face again. Then they accompanied him to the ship.

Paul Returns to Jerusalem

As we set sail and departed from them, we followed a straight course to Cos, and the day following to Rhodes, and from there to Patara, and having found a ship that was going over to Phoenicia, we went aboard and set sail. When Cyprus came into view, we kept it on the left hand and sailed toward Syria and arrived at Tyre, where the ship was to unload its cargo. When we had found disciples, we stayed there for seven days. They told Paul through the Spirit that he should not go up to Jerusalem. But when those days were ended, we departed and went our own way, and they all accompanied us out of the city, with their wives and children, and we kneeled down on the shore and prayed. After we had embraced one another, we took to the ship and they returned home.

When we had finished the voyage from Tyre, we arrived at Ptolemais and greeted the brethren and stayed with them one day. The next day, Paul and those of us with him departed and came to Caesarea, and we entered the house of Philip the evangelist, who was one of the seven deacons, and stayed with him. Now he had four virgin daughters who prophesied. And as we stayed there many days, a certain prophet from Judea came down named Agabus. And when he had come into us, he took Paul's belt and bound his own hands and feet and said, "This is what the holy Ghost says, 'So shall the Jews in Jerusalem bind the man who owns this girdle and will deliver him into the hands of the Gentiles.'" When we heard these things, we all begged him to not go up to Jerusalem. Then Paul answered and said, "What are you doing, weeping and breaking my heart? I am ready not only to be bound, but also to die in Jerusalem for the Name of the Lord Jesus." So when he would not be persuaded, we stopped and said, "The will of the Lord be done."

After those days we packed and went up to Jerusalem. Some of the disciples of Caesarea went with us, and brought with them one Mnason of Cyprus, an old disciple with whom we should lodge. And when we arrived in Jerusalem, the brethren received us gladly. And the next day Paul went in with us to James and all the elders were gathered there. And when he had embraced them, he told, in order, all the things that God had been working among the Gentiles through his ministry. When they heard it, they glorified God and said to him, "You see, brother, how many thousands of Jews there are which believe, and they are all zealous for the Law. They have been told about you, that you are teaching all the Jews who are among the Gentiles to forsake Moses, and that you are saying that they should neither circumcise their sons, nor obey the customs. What is to be done then? The assembly will certainly meet because they will hear that you have come. Therefore, do this which we tell you. We have four men who have made a vow, take them and purify yourself with them, and pay their expenses that they may shave their heads. Then all will know that the things they have heard about you are nothing, but that you yourself also walk and keep the Law. Concerning the Gentiles which believe, we have written and determined that they do no such thing, but that they keep themselves from things offered to idols, and from blood, and from what has been strangled, and from fornication." Then Paul took the men and was purified with them the next day, and entered into the temple, declaring the completion of the days of the purification and that an offering should be offered for each of them.

When the seven days were nearly ended, the Jews from Asia saw him in the Temple, and stirred up the people and laid hands on him, shouting, "Men of Israel, help; this is the man that is teaching all men everywhere against the people and the Law and this place. Furthermore, he has brought Greeks into the temple and has defiled this holy place." They had earlier seen him in the city with Trophimus, an Ephesian, and they supposed that Paul had brought him into the temple. Then the whole city was provoked and the people ran together, and they grabbed Paul and dragged him out of the temple, and immediately the doors were shut. But as they were going to kill him, news came to the commander of the cohort that all Jerusalem was in an uproar. He immediately took soldiers and centurions and ran down to them, and when they saw the commander and the soldiers, they stopped beating Paul. Then the commander came near and took hold of him, and ordered him to be bound with two chains, and demanded to know who he was and what he had done. And among all the people one shouted this and another that. When he could not determine the truth because of the uproar, he commanded him to be led into the garrison. When he came to the stairs, it was necessary for him to be carried by the soldiers because of the violence of the people, and the mob followed behind, crying, "Away with him."

As Paul was about to be led into the garrison, he said to the commander, "May I speak to you?" He said, "You can speak Greek? Are you not the Egyptian who some time ago started a revolution and led four thousand men that were assassins out into the wilderness?" Then Paul said, "I am a Jew from Tarsus in Cilicia, a citizen of an important city, and I beg you, allow me to speak to the people." And when he had given him permission, Paul stood on the stairs and motioned with his hand to the people, and when they became quiet, he spoke to them in Hebrew, saying: "Men, brothers and fathers, hear my defense before you now." When they heard that he spoke to them in Hebrew, they remained silent.

And he said, "I am a Jewish man, born in Tarsus in Cilicia, but brought up in this city under the teaching of Gamaliel and instructed in the perfect manner of the Law of the fathers, being zealous for God just as you all are today. I persecuted the Way to the death by binding and delivering both men and women into prison, as the chief priest and the council of the elders can testify, because I received letters from them to the brethren. I went to Damascus to capture those which were there, and to bring them to Jerusalem for punishment. And so it happened, as I journeyed, and had come near to Damascus about noon, that suddenly there shone from heaven a great light around me. I fell to the ground and heard a voice speaking to me, 'Saul, Saul, why are you persecuting me?' Then I answered, 'Who are you, Lord?' And he said to me, 'I am Jesus of Nazareth, whom you are persecuting.' Those that were with me indeed saw a light and were afraid, but they did not hear the voice of him that spoke to me. Then I said, 'What should I do, Lord?' And the Lord said to me, 'Get up, and go into Damascus. There you will be told of all things which are appointed for you to do.' Since I could not see because of the glory of that light, I was led by the hand by those with me and came into Damascus. And one Ananias, a godly man as pertaining to the Law and having a good reputation among all the Jews which dwelt there, came and stood by me and said to me, 'Brother Saul, regain your sight.' And immediately I could see him. Then he said, 'The God of our fathers has chosen you to know his will and to see the righteous One and to hear the voice of his mouth. You will be his witness to all men of the things which you have seen and heard. Now, why are you waiting? Get up and be baptized and wash away your sins by calling on the Name of the Lord.' Then it happened that after I had come again to Jerusalem and prayed in the temple, I was in a trance and saw him saying to me, 'Hurry and quickly get yourself out of Jerusalem because they will not believe your testimony about me.' Then I said, 'Lord, they know that I have imprisoned and beat those that believed in you in every synagogue; and that when the blood of your martyr Stephen was shed, I also stood by and consented to his death, guarding the coats of those who killed him.' Then he said to me, 'Depart, because I will send you to the Gentiles far from here.'"

They listened to him up to this point, but then they lifted up their voices and said, "Away with such a man from the earth; it is not right that he should live." As they shouted, they tore off their coats and threw dust into the air. The commander ordered him to be led into the garrison, saying that he should be flogged and questioned, so that he might know why they were shouting at him like this. And as they bound him with straps, Paul said to the centurion that stood by, "Is it lawful for you to flog one that is a Roman citizen and uncondemned?" Now when the centurion heard this, he went and told the commander, saying, "Be careful what you do because this man is a Roman." Then the commander came and said to him, "Tell me, are you a Roman?" And he said, "Yes." And the commander answered, "I obtained my citizenship with a large sum of money." Then Paul said, "But I was born a citizen." Then immediately those which were going to question him withdrew from him, and the commander was also afraid, after finding out that he was a Roman and that he had bound him. But since he wanted to know for certain why the Jews were accusing him, he let him go the next day and commanded that the high priests and all their council come together, and he brought Paul and put him before them.

Paul looked intently at the council and said, "Men and brothers, I have, in all good conscience, served God until this day." Then Ananias, the high priest, commanded those that stood nearby to strike him on the mouth. Then Paul said to him, "God will strike you, you whitewashed wall, because you sit in judgment over me according to the Law, and then you transgress the Law by commanding me to be struck?" And those that stood by said, "Do you insult God's high priest?" Then Paul said, "Brothers, I did not know that he was the high priest, for it is written, 'You shall not speak evil of the ruler of your people.'" But when Paul perceived that one part of the council were Sadducees and the other part Pharisees, he cried out in the council, "Men and brothers, I am a Pharisee, the son of a Pharisee, and I am on trial for the hope and resurrection of the dead." When he had said this, there was a dissension between the Pharisees and the Sadducees, so that the group was divided, because the Sadducees say that there is neither resurrection, nor angel nor spirit, but the Pharisees confess both. Then there was a great uproar and the scribes of the Pharisees' part stood up and protested, saying, "We find nothing wrong with this man. If a spirit or an angel has spoken to him, let us not fight against God." And as the dissension became greater and fearing that Paul might be pulled to pieces by them, the commander ordered the soldiers to go down and remove him from among them and to bring him into the garrison. And that night, the Lord stood by him and said, "Be of good courage, Paul, for just as you have testified about me in Jerusalem, so must you also testify in Rome."

When morning had come, some of the Jews got together and bound themselves with an oath, saying that they would neither eat nor drink until they had killed Paul; and there were more than forty which had conspired to do this. And they came to the chief priests and elders and said, "We have bound ourselves together with a solemn oath that we will eat nothing until we have slain Paul. Now therefore, you and the council request that the commander bring him to you tomorrow, saying that you want to question him more thoroughly, and when he comes near we will be ready to kill him. But when Paul's sister's son heard of their plot, he went and entered into the garrison and told Paul. Then Paul called one of the centurions to him and said, "Take this young man to the commander, because he has something to tell him." So he took him and brought him to the commander and said, "Paul the prisoner called me to him and asked me to bring this young man to you, because he has something to say to you." Then the commander took him by the hand and took him aside and asked him, "What do you have to tell me?" And he said, "The Jews have conspired to ask you to bring forth Paul tomorrow to the Council, as though they wanted to question him some more. But do not let them persuade you because more than forty men lie in wait for him, which have bound themselves with an oath that they will neither eat nor drink until they have killed him; and they are ready now, waiting for your consent." The commander let the young man depart after he had ordered him to tell no one that he had revealed it to him. And he called two centurions to him, saying, "Make ready two hundred soldiers, seventy horsemen, and two hundred spearmen to go to Caesarea at the third hour of the night. Then also prepare a horse for Paul to sit on so that he may be brought to Felix the governor safely." Then he wrote a letter to this effect:

> To the most noble governor Felix, Claudius Lysias sends greetings. This man was taken by the Jews and would have been killed by them if I had not come upon them with the soldiers and rescued him, realizing that he was a Roman. Since I wanted to know the reason why they accused him, I brought him unto their own council. There I understood that he was being accused over questions of their Law, but of no crime worthy of death or imprisonment. And when it was told to me that the Jews were lying in wait for the man, I sent him to you right away, and commanded his accusers to speak to you regarding the things that they had against him. *Farewell.*

Then as it was commanded of them, the soldiers took Paul and brought him to Antipatris by night. The next day, they left the horsemen to continue on with him and returned to the garrison. When they arrived in Caesarea, they delivered the letter to the governor and brought Paul before him. After the governor had read it, he asked what province he was from, and when he learned that he was from Cilicia, he said, "I will hear you when your accusers arrive." Then he commanded him to be kept in Herod's judgment hall.

Paul Before Felix and Festus

Now after five days, Ananias the high priest came down with the elders and with Tertullus a certain orator, and appeared before the governor against Paul. When he was called forward, Tertullus began to accuse him, saying, "We have obtained great peace because of you and many great things have been done for this nation through your provision; of this we fully acknowledge in every way and in every place and with all thankfulness, most noble Felix. But that I would not be wearying to you, I ask that you would kindly grant to listen to what we have to say. We have certainly found this man to be a plague and a creator of sedition among all the Jews throughout the world, and a leader of the sect of the Nazarenes. He even tried to defile the temple. Therefore we apprehended him, wanting to judge him according to our Law, but the comander Lysias came upon us, and with great violence took him out of our hands, commanding his accusers to come to you. And you may know these things for yourself if you will question him whom we are accusing." The Jews also agreed, affirming that it was so.

Then Paul, after the governor had motioned to him that he should speak, answered, "I am more than happy to answer for myself, because I know that you have been a judge of this nation for many years and so that you may know that it has been only twelve days since I came up to worship in Jerusalem. They neither found me in the temple disputing with any man, nor making uproar among the people, neither in the synagogues, nor in the city. Neither can they prove the things of which they are now accusing me. But I will confess this to you: After the Way, which they call heresy, do I worship the God of my fathers, believing everything which is written in the Law and the Prophets, having a hope in God that the resurrection of the dead—which they themselves also look for—shall be both of just and unjust. And in this, I endeavor to always have a clear conscience toward God and toward men. Now, after many years, I have come and brought charity to my nation and offerings; and at this time, some Jews from Asia found me purified in the temple, with neither a mob nor an uproar. They should be present before you accusing me, if they had anything against me. Or else let these say if they have found anything unjust in me when I stood before their council, other than this one thing that I shouted while standing among them, 'For the resurrection of the dead am I being accused by you today.'"

When Felix heard these things, he put them off and said, "When I shall understand better the things concerning this Way and when Lysias the commander comes, then I will decide your matter." Then he commanded a centurion to guard Paul, and that he should be comfortable and that none of his friends should be forbidden to minister to him or to visit with him. And after a few days, Felix came with his wife Drusilla, who was a Jew, and he called for Paul and listened to him about faith in Christ. But when he spoke of righteousness, self-control, and of the judgment to come, Felix became afraid and answered, "Go away for now and when it is convenient, I will call for you." He had been hoping that Paul would give him money so that he would release him; therefore he sent for him more often, and discussed with him. When two years had gone by, Porcius Festus succeeded Felix, and because he wanted to do the Jews a favor, Felix left Paul in prison.

When Festus arrived in the province, after three days he went up from Caesarea to Jerusalem. Then the high priest and the leaders of the Jews appeared before him, bringing charges against Paul; and they requested from him a favor against Paul: that he would have him brought to Jerusalem (and then they would ambush him along the way and kill him). But Festus answered that Paul would be kept in Caesarea, and that he himself would soon go there. "Therefore, let those which are able among you come down with us," he said, "and if there be any wickedness in the man, let them accuse him."

After he had stayed among them for no more than ten days, he went down to Caesarea, and the next day sat on the judgment seat and commanded that Paul be brought out. And when he had come, the Jews from Jerusalem stood around him, bringing many serious charges against him of which they had no proof. In his defense, Paul answered that he had neither offended anything against the law of the Jews, nor anything against the temple, nor against Caesar. Yet Festus wanted to get the favor of the Jews and answered Paul and said, "Will you go up to Jerusalem and be judged for these things before me there?" Then Paul said, "I stand before Caesar's judgment seat, where I ought to be judged. I have done nothing wrong to the Jews, as you know very well. If I have done wrong or committed anything worthy of death, I will not refuse to die; but if there is nothing to these things of which they accuse me, no man can deliver me to them to please them. I appeal to Caesar." Then after Festus had spoken with the council, he answered, "Have you appealed to Caesar? Then to Caesar you shall go."

After several days, King Agrippa and Bernice came down to Caesarea to greet Festus. And when they had been there many days, Festus discussed Paul's case with the king, saying, "There is a certain man left in prison by Felix, of whom the high priests and elders of the Jews told me when I came to Jerusalem, and desired to have a judgment against him. I told them that it was not the practice of the Romans to deliver any man over to death before the accused meets with his accusers and has a chance to defend himself concerning the crime. Therefore, when they came here and without delay, I sat on the judgment seat the following day and commanded the man to be brought out. And when the accusers stood up, they brought against him no charges of such things as I had thought, but they questioned him concerning their own religion, and of one Jesus which was dead, whom Paul affirmed to be alive. And because I was unsure of how to proceed with such questions, I asked him whether he would go to Jerusalem and be judged there of these accusations. But since he appealed and wanted to be questioned by Augustus, I commanded that he be guarded, until I can send him to Caesar." Then Agrippa said to Festus, "I would also like to hear the man myself." "Tomorrow," he said, "you shall hear him."

Paul Before Agrippa

The next day, when Agrippa and Bernice arrived with great pomp, and had entered into the common hall with the commanders and leading men of the city, they brought Paul out at Festus's command. And Festus said, "King Agrippa, and all men which are present with us, you see this man about whom all of the Jews have called upon me, both here and in Jerusalem, crying out that he should not live any longer. Yet I have found that he has committed nothing worthy of death. Nevertheless, since he has appealed to Augustus, I have determined to send him. But I have nothing certain to write to my lord about him, therefore I have brought him out to you and especially to you, King Agrippa, that after questioning him, I may have something to write. For I think it is unreasonable to send a prisoner and not to show the charges which have been brought against him."

Then Agrippa said to Paul, "You are permitted to speak for yourself." So Paul stretched out his hand and began defending himself. "I consider myself happy, King Agrippa, because I will answer before you today about all of the things of which I am accused by the Jews, mainly because you have understanding of all the customs and the questions which are among the Jews. Therefore I beg of you to listen to me patiently."

"Concerning my life from my childhood and what it was from the beginning among my own nation and at Jerusalem all the Jews know. They knew me from the beginning, even all the elders if they would admit it, that I lived according to the strictest sect of our religion, as a Pharisee. I now stand and am being accused because of the hope of the promise made by God to our fathers—the promise to which our twelve tribes hope to attain by earnestly worshiping God night and day. And for the sake of this hope, O King Agrippa, I am being accused by the Jews. Why should it be an incredible thought for you that God raises the dead again? I also had this very thought in myself, such that I purposed to do many contrary things against the Name of Jesus of Nazareth. Such things as I also did in Jerusalem, because having received authority from the high priests, I locked many in prison and when they were put to death, I gave my approval. I punished them throughout all the synagogues and forced them to blaspheme; and being furious against them, I persecuted them even into foreign cities."

"At this time, I was heading to Damascus with the authority and the commission of the high priests, and about midday, O king, I saw in the road a light from heaven even brighter than the sun shining around me and those which were with me. When we had all fallen to the earth, I heard a voice speaking to me and saying in Hebrew, 'Saul, Saul, why are you persecuting me? It is hard for you to kick against the prods.' Then I said, 'Who are you, Lord?' And he said, 'I am Jesus, whom you are persecuting. Get up and stand up on your feet because I have appeared to you for this purpose: to appoint you a minister and a witness, of both the things which you have seen and of the things which I will show to you. I will deliver you from the Jewish people and from the Gentiles, the ones to whom I am now sending you, in order to open their eyes and that they may turn from darkness to light, and from the power of Satan to God; that they may receive forgiveness for sins and an inheritance among those which are sanctified by faith in me.' Therefore King Agrippa, I was not disobedient to this heavenly vision, but declared first to those in Damascus, and in Jerusalem, and throughout all the coasts of Judea, and then to the Gentiles that they should repent and turn to God and do works worthy of a repentant life. For this reason, the Jews seized me in the temple and planned to kill me. Nevertheless, I received help from God and continue to this day, testifying to both small and to great, saying nothing other than what the Prophets and Moses said would come, meaning, that Christ would suffer and that he would be the first to rise from the dead, and would proclaim light to this people and to the Gentiles."

When he had answered for himself, Festus said with a loud voice, "Paul, you are out of your mind; much learning has made you mad." But he said, "I am not mad, O noble Festus, but I speak the words of truth and seriousness. For the king knows about these things, before whom I also speak boldly; I am convinced that none of these things are hidden from him, because this thing has not been done in a corner. King Agrippa, do you believe the Prophets? I know that you believe." Then Agrippa said to Paul, "You have almost persuaded me to become a Christian." Then Paul said, "I pray to God that not only you, but also all that hear me today, would become such as I am, except for these chains." And when he had said this, the king, the governor, Bernice, and those that sat with them, got up. And when they had dispersed, they talked amongst themselves, saying, "This man has done nothing worthy of death, nor of chains." Then Agrippa said to Festus, "This man might have been set free, if he had not appealed to Caesar."

Shipwrecked on Malta

When it was determined that we should sail to Italy, they brought Paul and some other prisoners to a centurion named Julius, who was from the regiment of Augustus. And we entered into a ship from Adramyttium, which was intending to sail along the coasts of Asia. We set to sea and Aristarchus, a Macedonian from Thessalonica, was with us. The next day we arrived at Sidon, and Julius treated Paul respectfully by giving him freedom to visit his friends and receive hospitality. And from there we set forth and sailed hard by Cyprus, because the winds were against us. Then we sailed over the sea by Cilicia and Pamphilia, and came to Myra, a city in Lycia. From there the centurion found an Alexandrian ship sailing to Italy and put us on it. After sailing slowly for many days, we had barely arrived at Cnidus because the wind did not allow us. Then we sailed hard by Candia, near to Salmone, and sailed beyond it with difficulty, and came to a certain place called Fair Havens, which was near the city of Lasea.

A considerable amount of time had passed and the sailing was now dangerous because of the time of the year, and Paul advised them and said to them, "Men, I perceive that this voyage will end with damage and great loss, not only to the cargo and the ship, but also to our lives." However, the centurion instead believed the captain and the owner of the ship, rather than the things which Paul had spoken. And because the harbor was not suitable to spend the winter, many advised them to leave there and to try and make it to Phoenix—which is a harbor off Crete, facing southwest and northwest—and spend the winter there. And when the southern wind began blowing gently, they supposed this would achieve their purpose and we set sail and sailed around Crete. But soon after, a stormy wind called Euroclydon rose up, and when the ship was caught and could no longer resist the wind, we let her go and got carried away. Then we ran under a little island named Clauda and with much difficulty secured the ship's boat. After hoisting it up, they took measures to undergird the ship, and fearing that they might run aground on Syrtis, they struck sail and so were carried. The next day, when we were being tossed violently by a strong wind, they lightened the ship. And the third day, we threw the ship's tackle overboard with our own hands. And when neither the sun nor the stars appeared for many days and the wind showed no sign of letting up, all hope that we would be saved was abandoned.

After a long time without food, Paul stood among them and said, "Men, you should have listened to me and should not have untied from Crete and incurred this damage and loss. But now I urge you to be of good courage, because there shall be no loss of any man's life among you, only of the ship. Last night, there stood next to me an angel of the God of whom I belong to and of whom I serve, saying, 'Do not fear Paul, because you must be brought before Caesar and God has freely granted unto you all those that are sailing with you.' Therefore, men, be of good courage because I believe God and it will happen just as it has been told to me. However, we will run aground on some island."

When the fourteenth night had come and we were being carried to and fro in the Adriatic Sea, around midnight the sailors sensed that they were nearing some land. And they took soundings and found it to be twenty fathoms; and when they had gone a little farther, they sounded again and found it to be fifteen fathoms. Fearing that they might run into the rocks, they threw four anchors off the stern, and prayed that morning would come. Then the sailors tried to flee the ship and began lowering the boat into the sea, pretending as though they were going to throw anchors off the bow. Then Paul said to the centurion and the soldiers, "Except they stay in the ship, you cannot be saved." So the soldiers cut the ropes of the boat and let it fall away.

As dawn was approaching, Paul urged all of them to eat, saying, "This is the fourteenth day that you have waited and gone without food, eating nothing. Therefore I encourage you to eat because this is for your preservation. Not one hair shall fall from the head of any one of you." And after he had said this, he took bread and gave thanks to God in front of all of them, and broke it and began to eat. Then they were all encouraged and also began to eat. In all, there were 276 of us on the ship. And after they had eaten enough, they lightened the ship and threw the wheat out into the sea. When it was morning, they did not recognize the land, but they found a bay with a beach, onto which they thought to direct the ship, if it were possible. When they had raised the anchors and committed the ship to the sea, they untied the ropes on the rudder and raised the main sail to the wind and began heading to the shore. And when they came to the place where the two waters met, they drove the ship in and the bow ran aground and could not be moved, but the stern began to break under the force of the waves. The soldiers' plan was to kill the prisoners, lest any of them should run away after he had swam out. But the centurion, willing to save Paul, stopped them from this plan and commanded that those that could swim should be the first to throw themselves into the water and head to land, while the others would come behind on boards and on pieces of the ship. And so it happened that all of them came safely to land.

After they were all safe, they found out that the island was called Malta. And the natives showed us much kindness; they built a fire and received everyone because it had begun to rain and it was getting cold. When Paul had gathered a number of sticks and laid them on the fire, a viper came out because of the heat and latched onto his hand. Now when the Barbarians saw the snake hanging on his hand, they said among themselves, "This man surely is a murderer, and though he has escaped from the sea, yet justice has not allowed him to live." But he shook the snake off into the fire and suffered no harm. But they were waiting for him to become swollen or suddenly fall down dead, and after they had watched him a long time and saw nothing unusual happen to him, they changed their minds and said that he was a god.

In the same region, the leading man of the island was named Publius. He had an estate and welcomed us, and courteously lodged us for three days. And it happened that Publius's father was sick with a fever and dysentery. Then Paul went in to him and after praying, he laid his hands on him and healed him. After this happened, others on the island who had diseases also came to him and were healed. They also showed us great honor, and when we were leaving, they supplied us with all that we needed.

Paul Arrives in Rome

After three months, we departed in an Alexandrian ship which had spent the winter on the island, whose sign was Castor and Pollux. When we arrived in Syracuse, we stayed there three days. From there we set a course and came to Rhegium, and a day later the south wind blew and on the second day we came to Puteoli. We found brothers there and decided to stay with them for seven days, and then we went toward Rome. From there, when the brethren heard about us, they came to meet us at the Market of Appius and at Three Taverns, and when Paul saw them, he thanked God and took courage. When we arrived in Rome, the centurion delivered the prisoners to the captain of the guard, but Paul was allowed to live by himself with the soldier who guarded him.

Three days later, Paul called the leading men of the Jews together, and when they had come, he said to them, "Men and brothers, though I have done nothing against our people or the Laws of the fathers, yet was I brought as a prisoner from Jerusalem into the hands of the Romans. They were willing to release me after questioning, because they found no grounds for putting me to death. But when the Jews spoke against me, I was forced to appeal to Caesar; it was not because I had anything of which to accuse my nation. Therefore, for this reason I have called for you to see you and to speak with you, because I am bound with this chain for the sake of the hope of Israel." Then they said to him, "We have not received letters from Judea concerning you, neither did any of the brethren that came here show or speak any evil towards you. But we would like to hear from you what you think, because with regards to this sect, we know that it is being spoken against everywhere."

And when they had set a day for him, many were coming to him in his lodging, and he explained and testified about the kingdom of God, persuading them of the things concerning Jesus—both from the Law of Moses and from the Prophets—from morning to night. And some were persuaded by the things which were being spoken, but some would not believe. Therefore since they could not agree among themselves, they began to depart after Paul had spoken this word to them: "The holy Ghost spoke well by Isaiah the prophet to our fathers when he said, 'Go to this people and say, "By hearing you shall hear and shall not understand, and seeing you shall see and not perceive. The heart of this people has grown fat and their ears are hard of hearing and their eyes they have closed, lest they should see with their eyes and hear with their ears, and understand with their hearts, and return so that I might heal them."' Therefore let it be known to you that this salvation of God is sent to the Gentiles, and they will hear it." After he had said this, the Jews departed and had great disputes among themselves. And Paul remained for two full years, living in a rented house, welcoming all that came to him, and preaching the kingdom of God and teaching those things concerning the Lord Jesus Christ with all boldness and without hindrance.